PEOPLES OF THE EARTH

volume one
Australia and Melanesia
(including New Guinea)

THE DANBURY PRESS

(Preceding spread) towheaded young aborigines play near Ernabella mission, South Australia. Soon their hair will turn black and their play turn to seeking food.

Publisher
ROBERT B. CLARKE
Marketing Director
ROBERT G. BARTNER
Creative Director
GILBERT EVANS

© 1972

Tom Stacey and Europa Verlag

Library of Congress Catalog Card No. 72 85614

Printed in Italy by
Arnoldo Mondadori Editore, Verona

PHOTOGRAPHIC CREDITS

Cover – **David Moore** (Black Star New York), **David Moore** (Daily Telegraph), **David Beal** (Daily Telegraph), **John Bulmer**. 2, 3 – **David Moore** (Daily Telegraph). 14, 15 – **David Moore** (Black Star New York). 16 – **Ted Spiegel** (Rapho New York), **David Beal**. 17 – **Jeffrey Craig**. 18 – **Ted Spiegel** (Rapho New York), **David Beal**. 19 – **Thomas Höpker** (The John Hillelson Agency); bot. rt. **David Moore** (Black Star New York). 20, 21 – **David Moore** (Black Star New York); top rt. **Ted Spiegel** (Rapho New York); bot. rt. **Tor Eigeland** (Black Star New York). 22, 23 – **Ted Spiegel** exc. top cen. (**FPG**.) 24, 25 – **FPG**. 26 – **Thomas Höpker** (The John Hillelson Agency), **David Moore** (Black Star New York). 27 – **Ted Spiegel** (Rapho New York). 28, 29, 31 – **David Moore** (Black Star New York). 33 – **David Moore** (Black Star New York), **Ted Spiegel** (Rapho New York). 34 – **John Marmaras** (Daily Telegraph), **Thomas Höpker** (The John Hillelson Agency). 35, 36 – **Thomas Höpker** (The John Hillelson Agency). 37 – **David Moore** (Black Star New York). 38, 39 – **John Marmaras** (Woodfin Camp New York) exc. bot. rt. **John Marmaras** (Daily Telegraph). 40, 41 – **FPG**. 42 – **FPG** exc. top lt. **J. and P. Villeminot**. 44, 45 – **Axel Poignant**. 46, 47 – **Axel Poignant** exc. top rt. **David McKnight**. 48 through 53 – **Richard A. Gould**. 55 – **National Library of Australia**. 56 – **National Library of Australia** exc. bot. lt. **Axel Poignant**. 58, 59 – **Axel Poignant**. 60, 61 – **Jane C. Goodale** (FPG). 64 through 69 – **Tony Saulnier**. 70 through 79 – **Anthony Forge**. 80 through 87 – **Klaus-Friedrich Koch**. 88 through 91 – **Burt Glinn** (Magnum from the John Hillelson Agency). 92 through 99 – **Robert Gardner**. 100, 101 – **J. and P. Villeminot**. 102, 103, 104 – **Robin Smith** (FPG). 195 – **J. and P. Villeminot** exc. cen. **M. W. Young**. 108, 109, 110 – **Eliot Elisofon** (FPG). 111 – **FPG**. 112, 113, 114, 115 – **David Moore** (FPG). 116, 117, 118 – **Kal Muller**. 119 – **Kal Muller** exc. top lt. **Camera Press**. 120 through 132 – **Kal Muller**.

Contents

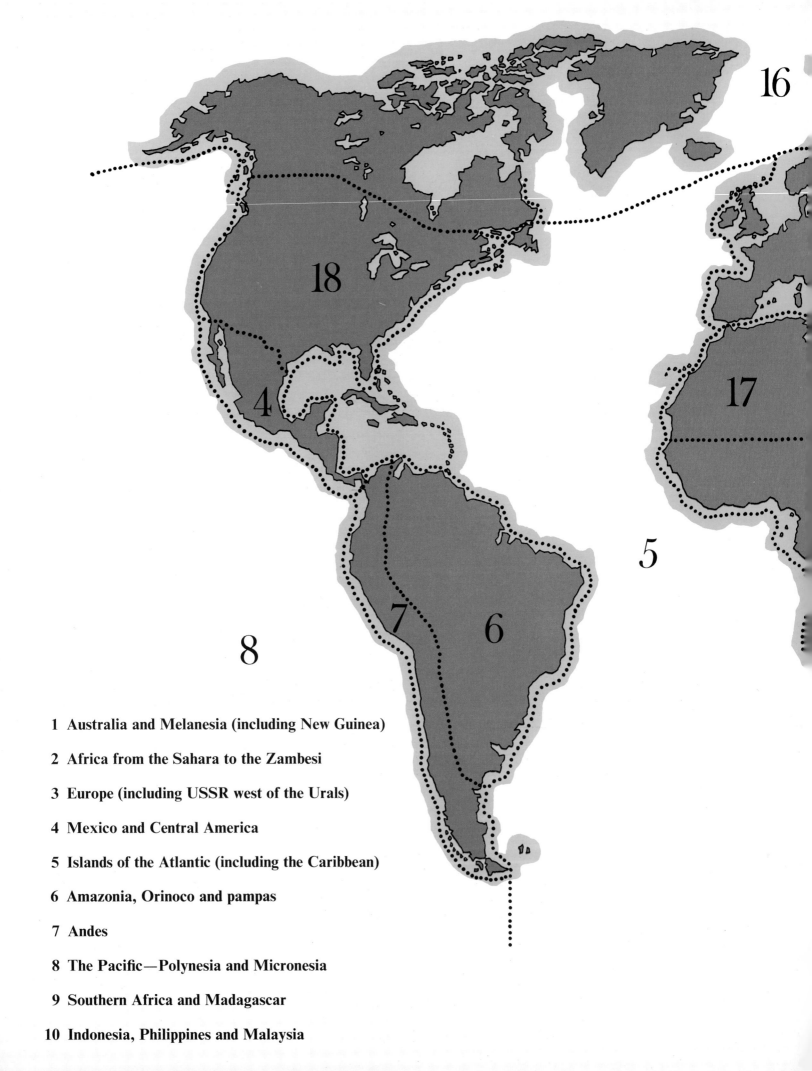

1 **Australia and Melanesia (including New Guinea)**

2 **Africa from the Sahara to the Zambesi**

3 **Europe (including USSR west of the Urals)**

4 **Mexico and Central America**

5 **Islands of the Atlantic (including the Caribbean)**

6 **Amazonia, Orinoco and pampas**

7 **Andes**

8 **The Pacific—Polynesia and Micronesia**

9 **Southern Africa and Madagascar**

10 **Indonesia, Philippines and Malaysia**

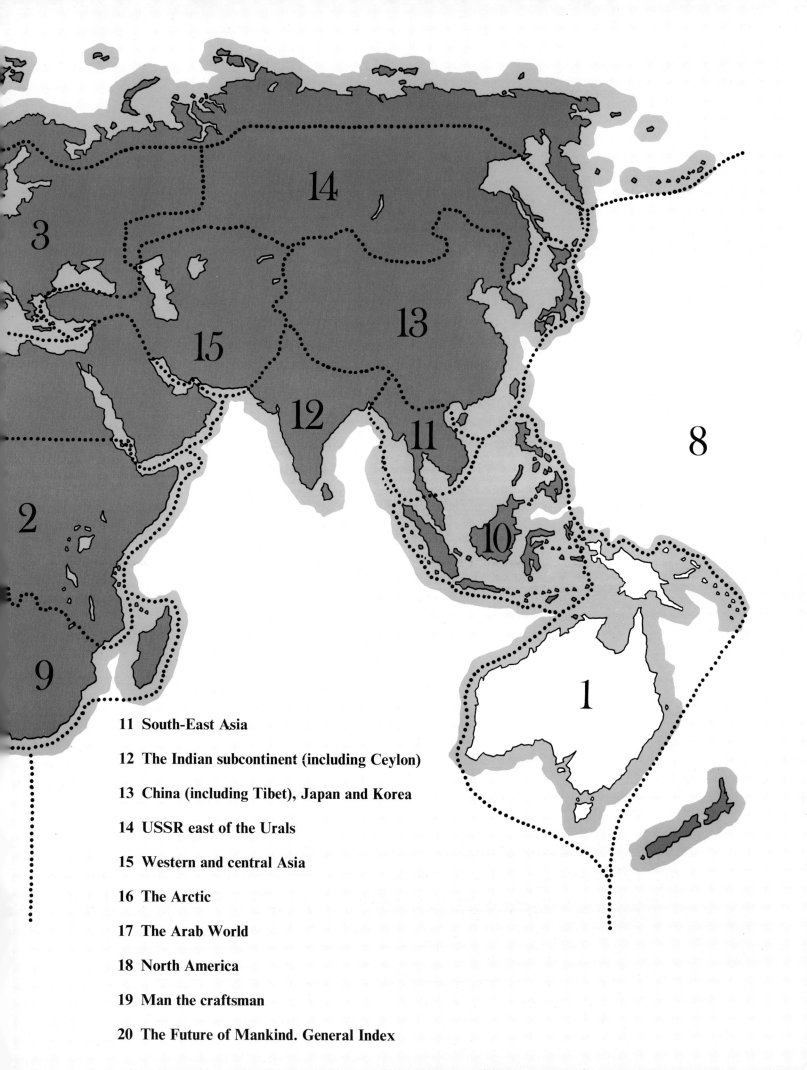

A message from the Supervisory Editor of the series

The proper study of mankind is man
ALEXANDER POPE 1688-1744

Earlier attempts to present to general readers a rounded picture of the peoples and cultures of the world have long been shown to have been inadequate and inaccurate by the very great amount of research which has been carried out during the last fifty or so years by anthropologists, ethnologists and ethnographers. There is no work available which can compare in comprehensiveness and authority with the twenty volumes of this series, which set forth, with a minimum of technical jargon, the harvest of these researches and discoveries.

Over the past few years anthropology has become a subject of interest to an ever widening public, due no doubt in part to man's broadening horizons and in part to the increasing ease and swiftness in travel and communication. But it may also be in part due to the feeling many have that the blessed diversity of humankind is being extinguished by the dominant technological culture of the West and that much is thereby being lost to the spirit of man. Much is indeed being lost, but much can yet be saved, as these volumes, written by persons well qualified to know the facts and express judgments on them, show. This is not just, or purely, a scientific matter; it is also a moral issue. It is right for us all to learn that no one people or group of peoples can claim the river of truth. All, some more and some less it is true, have contributed to its waters.

The object of this unique series of volumes has been to make it possible for the general reader to learn for the first time on a global scale about peoples, both large and small, as they are today or have recently been. The series covers peoples representing every level of technological culture, from hunters and collectors, still using stone tools, to the inhabitants of industrial cities, living as most of us

Consulting Editors of the series

ROBERT ARDREY
author of *African Genesis*, etc.

Professor ROBERT J BRAIDWOOD
Oriental Institute, University of Chicago, author of *Prehistoric Men*

Professor ROBIN FOX
Rutgers University, author of *Pueblo Ethnology*

THOR HEYERDAHL
leader of the *Kon-Tiki* and *Ra* expeditions, author of *Aku-Aku: The Secrets of Easter Island*

today live, with all our comforts and yet also with all our strains and tensions as well.

Those humble peoples whose very survival is threatened are given as much attention as are those great nations which occupy whole continents. Here are demonstrated, in page after page, the fascinating differences between various types of men and the enormous variety of territorial and climatic circumstances in which they live, which in turn have produced a great variety of solutions and adjustments. A good deal of exaggeration, even of rubbish, certainly of prejudice, has been written in the past about peoples outside the West, and especially about what were called 'savage' or 'barbarous' peoples. This set of volumes aims at simply presenting the facts, insofar as they are known and, as the text and the thousands of pictures in color and black and white demonstrate, the facts speak for themselves and are fascinating enough.

The publication of these volumes is, I believe, an important contribution to our understanding of one another. If we are to live together in harmony this can only be done by our tolerance of each other and tolerance is brought about, if not entirely, at least largely, through knowledge of the ways of life, the sentiments, the values and the beliefs of other peoples. They may not be ours, but when we know what they are we can respect them as theirs, as they can respect ours as ours.

E. E. Evans - Pritchard.

Professor Sir Edward Evans-Pritchard, M.A., Ph.D.
Fellow of All Souls, Professor of Social Anthropology, University of Oxford, 1946-1970
Chevalier de la Légion d'Honneur
Supervisory Editor of the series

Dr EDMUND LEACH
Provost, King's College, Cambridge, author of *Rethinking Anthropology*, etc.

Dr L S B LEAKEY
Professor at Large Cornell University, author of *Stone-Age Customs of Kenya,* etc.

Dr DESMOND MORRIS
Curator of Mammals, Zoological Society of London (1959-1967), author of *The Naked Ape*, etc.

Dr JACQUES SOUSTELLE
author of *The Ancient Civilisations of Mexico*, etc.

The Question of Human Conservation

When anthropology first became an academic subject, the myths and customs of savages were thought to have existed more or less unchanged from primordial times. True, some savages were more primitive than others. True, also, many had become civilized, and in course of time became capable of speculating on the origins of mankind! Soon, anthropologists became more interested in how tribal societies used their traditions and in the principles that governed the function of more or less coherent societies, rather than in evolutionary theory.

Then, as contact between western and tribal societies became more frequent, it became harder to find out how things once had been, because all was changing: the study of social change became necessary, and later the sociology of the apocalypse. Few anthropologists, however, have tried their hands at describing the death of a tribe: it is a mournful subject at best, and the art of delivering a funeral oration has itself suffered a decline. Yet now is the time when tribal cultures are dying all around us, and at an ever increasing rate. There are so many different kinds of tribal organization, making the best of such different conditions, that we can only generalize about the whys and wherefores.

For a start, let us take it that a tribe has institutions based on the idea of family relationship, and that non-tribal man has found another social logic by which to exist. Even to ourselves, this logic is incoherent, indiscriminate and unsatisfactory: its effect on tribal peoples is all too understandable, and the rapid and often fatal change they are undergoing faces us with the problem of our responsibility to them. Can we, who now hear voices telling us that the family itself is at the root of all human troubles, help those who successfully held the opposite view, but are now coming to resemble us?

When Europeans first landed on the coast of Brazil, they found many and populous tribes, whose outlandish customs were a matter both for curiosity and disapproval. It was not long before the Portuguese had tamed the cannibalistic Tupi-speaking tribes, using the traditional device of allying themselves with one group to put paid to another. The client tribes were then variously missionized, enslaved if possible, or killed off, their remnants disappearing into the hinterland and dislocating the tribal orders which existed there. Pioneers followed them, exploring and exploiting the interior; the forests were felled, roads and railways built, settlements, plantations and industries sprang up. The Indians, whose societies were politically weak and whose chiefship was not well developed, were unable either to absorb or challenge this invasion. Like the last of the Inca, who were so much better equipped, they retreated further into the wilderness if they could, or if not, suffered all the indignities of being outside the law but within the power of their oppressors.

The first effort at dealing with the Indians in an honorable fashion came when telegraph lines were strung through the interior, and the Service for the Protection of Indians was founded under General Rondon. Its aim was to pacify the tribes without bloodshed, using gifts, understanding and kindness instead; its success was great, and we can only mourn its ultimate failure. This was as much due to poor administration and lack of funds as to the greed of speculators. For Brazil is now repeating the

Francis Huxley

course America followed in the last century. It is taking hold of its territory in no uncertain fashion, and the wilderness is being parcelled out and developed on a large scale, sometimes with a plan, often blindly. And the Indian population is steadily going down.

In 1963 their numbers were estimated at some 200,000, which is but a small fraction of their strength before the fifteenth century; by 1968 this number had shrunk to 80,000, and in 1971 to 50,000. Most of these Indians are already pacified, either by the old SPI of the new foundation, FUNAI, or by missionaries. Some of them have little to complain of, others a great deal, for many are but jungle slum dwellers, in debt bondage to those they work for, prostituted by passing lorry drivers, abused by the peasantry, and in general treated as pariahs. There also remain a few small and lonely tribes, who seem to know all too well what is in store for them if they lose their independence.

Though some tribes, like the Trio, have kept up their numbers, the general decline in population cannot be argued away. It is true that the peasant population has Indian blood in it, and that Indian myths have become stock superstitions amongst Brazilians: in this way, it has been said, Indians have become assimilated into the nation. If this is true, and there are many reasons to think otherwise, they have become assimilated in the unhappiest and most one-sided way imaginable, by rape rather than by intermarriage.

The reasons for the decline are plain enough. Indians speak their own languages, have bizarre customs, defend themselves when attacked – indeed, sometimes they attack first – and are exotic to those who come in contact with them. To be exotic is to be alien and out of context. It is no surprise, therefore, that aboriginal peoples are seldom thought of as assets to a country, even when – as in Brazil – they taught the first colonists how to live off the land, the crops to use, the fruit and nuts to gather, and the names and uses of plants and animals. In spite of this they remain outside the pale of society and of law and order, and can be dealt with as one pleases.

They are also prone to die of common and to us non-fatal diseases. Eskimo have died in epidemics of the common cold: Amerindians of measles and influenza, having neither a natural immunity to nor traditional remedies for such diseases. The epidemics may be started by visiting traders, prospectors, missionaries and social anthropologists, or by the Indians themselves who have gone visiting neighboring townships. Medicines are hard to come by in the interior, doctors are scarce, and preventable fatalities amongst the Indians many.

We could come to quite similar conclusions about other tribal peoples. Many of them, like the Bushmen, are not decreasing in numbers, only in the ability to fend for themselves: a class of miserable and detribalized human beings has been created amongst them, who will soon pose as much of a problem to the countries they live in as they now do to themselves. In the Pacific, messianic movements are a problem to the authorities, who imprison the leaders on charges of treason. The Tasmanians have all been killed off, but the Australian Aborigines survived, and they are now beginning to clamor for their rights. It might have been easier if they had been given their rights in the first place.

But some tribes are more fragile than others. Should we try to save them from extinction, as we are trying to save the oryx, the tiger, the Japanese crane? The matter is not that simple: tribes breed culture as well as progeny, and it is exactly the difference between cultures which militates against their survival. Some politicians argue that progress is inevitable, and that tribal man will die out whatever we do. They may be right. They also argue against putting tribes into reservations, or as they like to call them now, human zoos.

Reservations are indeed not a final answer, as we can see from the fate of reservation Indians in North America. Nor can any human beings be kept like animals: they are as curious and inventive as we are, given the chance, expect to be made privy to the goods and values of our civilization, and resent it if they are kept out. We cannot legislate against change, we can only try to make it understandable, a matter of promise rather than of despair.

Margaret Mead has argued from her work on the islands of Manus that it is best to change from a tribal to a modern style of life as quickly as possible: we should, as it were, send a tribe to school and make it pass its examinations in a single generation. This may indeed be the most expedient method where the technical means lie ready to hand, even if most of the family heirlooms must be abandoned. For change, at least, is inevitable. Give a man a steel axe and his world is transformed: instead of spending days clearing the bush, and having to ask his neighbors to help him, he can do the work himself in a third of the time. The old system of co-operation goes by the board, individual notions of property become the rule, the elders are no longer at the center of things, and the tradition loses its meaning.

There is no way of preserving a human culture except to pickle it in a book, a tape, a film, a museum. We should certainly do this: indeed, just over a decade ago Dr Heine-Geldern founded the Bulletin for Urgent Anthropological Research, and began to list tribes in danger of passing away before they had been systematically investigated. Such information is of value not only to ourselves – certain of our sciences and many of our arts have been greatly influenced by tribal modes of thought – but to the tribes themselves, for unless we know in good time and in some detail how they are threatened, we have little chance of doing anything practical for them. And if a tribe is already *in extremis*, to record their traditions is an honorable way of paying tribute to them, and not to be despised.

But what is one to do when a road is built across a tribal area, or an industry set up there to extract minerals? Governments have a duty to increase the health and prosperity of their citizens, and when the fate of a small tribe is put in the balance against the material advancement of a nation, it is understandable that the tribe will lose out. We can only suggest that there are a number of immediate and interim measures which will give tribal peoples time in which to come to terms with their situation. If they are to be moved from their old haunts for political or economic reasons which cannot be gainsaid – civilized man suffers the same fate when a motorway or a redevelopment scheme ousts him from his home – they must at least be compensated, given new lands and legal rights to them.

Landrights for tribal peoples can be a vexing

problem. Many countries have already passed statutes granting them such titles, a matter easier to arrange for agricultural than for nomadic tribes. Even with settled tribes, however, there is a problem: is the title to be given to the tribe as a whole, or to its members? Or should the title be held in trust for them, until their ideas of property have caught up with ours? In addition, it is one thing to put laws on the statute book, another to see they are carried out, or that the beneficiaries are aware of their rights. Who is to do this, if the tribe cannot do so itself? Here looms the specter of paternalism, and the often unfortunate behavior of landowners, colonial officers and their ilk, missionaries, traders and others. In the absence of any other familial relationship in which tribal and non-tribal man can meet, however, we may have to make the most of paternalism where it exists, for there is often nothing else to make use of. The Villas Boas brothers of Amazonia

are, of course, a famous and shining exception to the paternalistic rule, and it is only because of their arduous and sensitive endeavors that the Xingu National Park came into being, and still exists.

The Park was founded, we must recall, on a pre-existent Indian institution, a ceremonial federation uniting a number of small tribes who had found refuge there, and the aim of the Park is to introduce other tribes into this federation and to foster its development until it can take care of itself. Whether the idea is politically tolerable in the long run, and whether it can be used in other parts of the world, remains to be seen. There are other men, in Brazil as in the rest of the world, as devoted to their work with tribal peoples as the Villas Boas brothers, though often unknown; and it is clear that if tribal disasters are to be staved off, it is such men who should be in charge of the operation.

There are now many bodies in Europe and the United States that are trying to organize such operations – from the outside. They rightly draw attention to what is being lost to the world as tribes die out, and have to consider such problems as have been outlined above. The help they can give can range all the way from the local to the international level: they can provide medical help, technical experts, equipment, and can put their hands to the political levers available to them. Faced with the death of their raw material, anthropologists may be forced to turn their theories into practice, the ultimate test of all knowledge. There are more pressing problems: but if the world is worth saving as a whole, some effort to save a small part of it will not be misplaced.

White Australia

The four children of this family got their basic education over the radio link, which is many a farm's life-line.

The outstanding French political scientist André Siegfried flattered Australia by studying it. His was an acute mind. And he said a startling thing: 'A mystery broods over this continent, and it will not be the economists who will resolve it for us.' The essential traditions of Australia are derived from Britain. What confuses is the fact that in Australia the four communities of the British Isles are mixed in different proportions. It is the relatively greater abundance of the Scottish, Welsh and Irish elements in the Australian tradition, and the relatively less significance of the English, which provide the background to Australian life.

Up to 1930, migration to Australia was almost entirely from the British Isles. For the next 15 years there was little migration of any kind. Since 1946 the rate of immigration has been high. While Britain is still the largest single source of migrants, other countries are now making substantial contributions to the total – in particular Italy, the Netherlands, Greece and Poland.

The culture and customs of these countries are beginning to be felt in Australian life. But the distinction is emphatically not one between Celtic and Anglo-Saxon stock, in the unscientific language of Victorian crypto-racialists. There is an obstinate belief in Australia that Southern Italians are of a different (and inferior) 'race' to North Italians. What Australians are observing, of course, is not race but a tradition, ingrained over many generations, of the inferior culture of the South.

Climatically, the mainland of Australia belongs to two different worlds, which become three when we take into account Tasmania, where the climate closely resembles England's. Southern New South Wales, Victoria, and the inhabited parts of South Australia and West Australia live under what the geographers call a 'Mediterranean' climate, very similar to that of Spain or Italy. There is adequate rainfall, mostly falling in the winter months, followed by a hot dry summer. Wheat grows well in this climate, and is harvested early; the same is true of those traditional symbols of the Mediterranean culture, the vine, the olive and the orange. The dry summer makes intensive livestock farming more difficult, though by no means impossible.

Queensland and northern New South Wales, on the other hand live under a sharply contrasted climate, known to geographers as 'monsoonal.' This climate, of hot humid summers with regular heavy rainfall, followed by a dry winter and spring, is like that of southern Asia, Central America, and most of Africa. In monsoonal Australia some sugar cane but hardly any rice or maize are grown; most of the land is used for cattle. Central New South Wales is intermediate between the two climatic types.

Both the Mediterranean and the monsoonal lands shade out into semi-arid and arid lands as you proceed northwards and westwards. It is a completely mistaken belief that Australia is a vast desert surrounded by a small 15

White Australia

Australia's White population is concentrated in a handful of cities — though agriculture remains a vital industry.

URBAN POPULATION

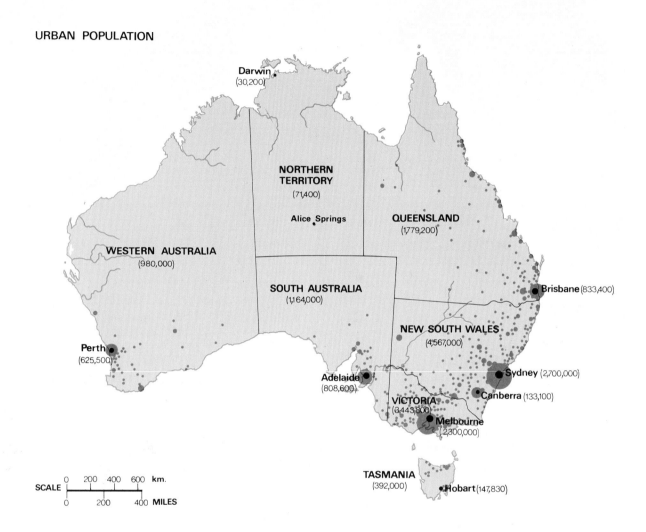

Darwin
(30,200)

NORTHERN
TERRITORY
(71,400)

Alice Springs

QUEENSLAND
(1,779,200)

WESTERN AUSTRALIA
(980,000)

SOUTH AUSTRALIA
(1,164,000)

Brisbane (833,400)

NEW SOUTH WALES
(4,567,000)

Perth
(625,500)

Sydney (2,700,000)

Adelaide
(808,600)

Canberra (133,100)

VICTORIA
(3,443,800)

Melbourne
(2,300,000)

TASMANIA
(392,000)

Hobart (147,830)

SCALE

| 0 | 200 | 400 | 600 | km. |

| 0 | 200 | 400 | MILES |

Australian race-goers do not normally dress up. The Melbourne Cup Race is different: an occasion for hats and champagne.

American buffalo, first brought to Australia in the 1820s, are still hunted for their hides by men like this.

The great-granddaughter of
an Australian pioneer stands
on the verandah of a fine
'squattocracy' house in York,
Western Australia.

White Australia

rim of habitable land. The amount of true desert, i.e. land lacking in vegetation, is limited. Even if we include the land categorized by geographers as arid, it still only covers about one-third of the map. There are substantial areas whose geographical description is semi-arid. These, and the arid areas to a less extent, can, and do, provide pasture for substantial numbers of sheep and cattle. Cattle are found to stand up to rough and arid conditions better than sheep – they can last longer between drinks.

Even those who know the least of biology (and most Australians are quite well informed in this field) are aware of the extraordinary differentiation of Australian flora and fauna from those of the rest of the world. People who will rarely venture into those regions where the kangaroo and the emu can be seen in their native habitat are firmly attached to them as national symbols. Australia has birds which bear only a partial resemblance to their European counterparts (for instance, the Australian magpie has a beautiful singing voice), reptiles including poisonous snakes in abundance, but no native mammals except the marsupials – kangaroos and wallabies – who all carry their young in pouches. (The dingo, or wild dog, was almost certainly introduced by man, although a long time ago.) Other Australian creatures – the furry, duck-billed platypus and the echidna, another egg-laying mammal – break all rules of biological classification.

The trees, predominantly but not entirely various species of eucalyptus, are quite distinct from those of the rest of the world. One of the great mysteries of biology is 'Wallace's line,' a biological line which winds in and out among the Indonesian archipelago, often separating islands only a few miles apart. On one side of the line the flora and fauna are completely Asian, and on the other side completely Australian.

These climatic and biological influences lie at the back of the Australian mind. Australian history, short though it has been, has had much more clearly marked effects. It is well known that the colonization of Australia began as a convict settlement. The convicts lived under conditions which were very harsh – but so were those of eighteenth century prisons. And transportation did at least give a substantial proportion of them the opportunity to rehabilitate themselves, which seems to be a regrettably rare outcome for those who go to prison in the modern world. The extent of the convict element in Australian ancestry is, however, very small – if for no other reason than because of the comparative scarcity of women.

South Australia was never a convict settlement. It was governed under charter, by a group of pedants in London who planned, unsuccessfully, to compel the inhabitants to form comparatively small holdings, and thus raise the price of land. It was said for a long time that a certain smugness could be detected in South Australians. In colloquial Australian, South Australians are addressed as 'crow-eaters' (South Australia has a number of German settlers, and crow-eating was an ancient German custom,

18

From cramped, urban West European family origins beach boys like Greek gods exemplify young Australia's immense physical confidence.

Tests of manhood for the young Sydneysider are supplied by the Pacific surf and sharks — and a life-saver's skill.

Australia is a vast continent but most of white Australia lives by the sea — either in the big cities or in suburbs like this.

19

White Australia

Sugar cane is burned to
remove the sharp leaves and
drive out the snakes before
harvesting at Murwillumbah,
New South Wales.

20

The traditional method of
hand-cutting the cane for
Australia's big sugar
industry is being replaced
by mechanical cane harvesters.

German settlers brought Lutheranism to Australia — as to this mixed 'Abo' and white congregation near Alice Springs.

as St. Boniface complained when he first went to civilize them). In the same language, West Australians are sand-gropers, New South Welshmen corn-stalks, and Queenslanders, banana-landers.

Much more important than the existence of the convicts, who left few descendants, was the fact that Australia, in its earliest and most formative years, was under rigid military government. Australia, unhappily, is still a highly bureaucratized community. Australians grumble, but put up with it. Traditions, however, do sometimes tend to breed their opposite. The legend, or rather the actual history, of the 'Gold Rush' in the brand new state of Victoria in the 1850s still exerts a powerful influence on the Australian consciousness. It keeps alive the gambling instinct, and the undying hope that even the poorest and most unsuccessful may some day 'strike it rich.'

The diggers raised the cry of 'no taxation without representation' and in 1854, at the township of Eureka, they armed themselves and threw up a fortified stockade. The Governor ordered the troops to attack, and the stockade was captured with the loss of 30 lives. Apart 21

Neat bungalows and lovingly watered jacarandas speak of surburban conformity, which combines with Australia's pioneer excitement.

White Australia

Saatas planes, typical of those used by the flying doctor and ambulance services, come in to land at Alice Springs airport in the Northern Territory.

Leading his only form of transport, a traditional prospector heads into the Simpson Desert, central Australia, in search of gold.

An enthusiastic ringside spectator attempts to participate in this amateur boxing bout in Burnie, Tasmania.

from primitive battles among the aborigines, the battle of the Eureka Stockade is the only armed conflict which has ever occurred on Australian soil. The Eureka legend has a strong hold on the Australian consciousness. When the Communists became a force in Australian politics (as they are to this day) they shrewdly named their youth organization 'Eureka Youth League.'

The term 'digger' survived from this period as a title of honor. It was almost universally used by Australian soldiers at the time of the First World War, although it is now disappearing. But a countryman will still often address his friend as 'digger.' A less creditable reaction against the bureaucratic tradition was that of the 'bush-rangers,' who in any other country would have been called bandits, except that they were not organized in large gangs. The remoteness of the country and the lack of communications enabled them to elude the police and soldiers until as late as the 1880s, when bush-ranging finally disappeared. (Cattle rustling however occurs to this day in some isolated areas.)

One of the last and best known of the bush-rangers was Ned Kelly. Kelly, a bandit in home-made armor, was undoubtedly a violent man, but his contemporaries admired his courage, and there was a considerable petition for his reprieve. Australia has not had a crime record anything like that of the United States, either in the nineteenth century or now. But the dream of forcible defiance of authority, Ned Kelly style, is still quite strong in the Australian mind.

It is one of the truisms which people tend to forget, that the entire peopling of Australia, apart from the Aborigines, depended upon migration. But the Australian's attitude towards migration has often been somewhat ambivalent, with a 'Here am I. Shut the door after me,' attitude. There is an exclusive club in Sydney whose members have to prove that their ancestors arrived in Australia before 1823 – and of their own accord.

The Australian is uncertain in his feelings even towards migrants coming from the same country as himself. But the really burning issue arose when the migrants were of a different color, or of what was believed to be a different race. Chinese came in large numbers to the gold fields which were discovered all over Australia in the nineteenth century. Most of them did not intend to stay permanently, but hoped to make some money and retire to 'the flowery land.' Their conduct was generally exemplary; but before long there were vicious anti-Chinese riots.

Most of the world thinks that the 'White Australia' policy is still in force, so slowly does news travel. It remained in force as long as Sir Robert Menzies was Prime Minister. But in 1966 his successor, Holt, immediately altered course, and began admitting Asians, in strictly limited numbers – a policy adopted by Canada and the United States 20 years earlier. The present administration is still admitting Asians, but very slowly and awkwardly and earning considerable ill-will. Migra-

23

A sampler of claret, ageing in oak casks at Barossa Valley, South Australia, tests this wine for bottling.

Bowls is not only a game but
something of a ritual, which
at Bondi, Sydney, demands
white ducks and dresses.

Bowls is not only a game but something of a ritual, which at Bondi, Sydney, demands white ducks and dresses.

tion to Australia came in great waves, in the 1880s, in the later Edwardian periods, and to a less extent in the 1920s. As soon as the trade unions and the Australian Labour Party became strong enough to play an active part in Australian affairs, they recorded their opposition, not only to Asian, but to all migration.

Australian rural life is split by a division which seems to go right back to the days of Cain and Abel. This is the irrational contempt which the grazier feels for the man who actually works the soil. In other English-speaking countries 'farmer' is an honorable and sought-after appellation; to call an Australian grazier a farmer is to offer him a vile insult. Conversely, the word 'squatter,' in other English-speaking countries, has the highly pejorative meaning of someone who occupies property which does not belong to him; in Australia it is a deeply respected title.

When the land was largely unexplored, and there were no legal titles, the early settlers occupied the land first, and obtained legal confirmation later, and often ended up wealthy men. A number of them were sons of English landowning families, debarred from inheritance by the Law of Entail, sent out to Australia with a little money, considerable education and taste, and a general willing-

ness to try almost anything once.

They were contemptuous of the poor 'cocky' farmers who came later, and who tried to use political influence to obtain land. ('Cocky' is an abbreviation for cockatoos; they were so called because they came in such numbers, and tried to pick the best of the land.) Apart from the social harm done by these distinctions, such irrational and deep-seated prejudices have caused great economic damage. Much of the comparatively low rainfall land held in grazing holdings would be capable of some measure of cultivation, greatly increasing its productivity.

What about the Australian business world? Its condition can be summed up in a single sentence. Making money is far too easy, and few businessmen therefore show much effort or enterprise. Or, in formal language, there is not enough competition. This is partly due to natural circumstances – in a small and remote city there may be very few suppliers of a commodity or service, so they can easily combine in a trade agreement, or form a local monopoly. But the situation has been brought about mainly by two definite Government actions, the establishment of tariff protection, and the absence of any effective legislation against restrictive practices in business. The Australian attitude is that, while governments

A prospector weighs gold in
the traditional manner.
Most goldmining is now in
the hands of the big
companies.

are unavoidably bureaucratic, they are also Father Christmas, whose duty is to hand out presents in return for getting elected.

And the manual wage workers? Nineteenth century Australia, long before the days of Labour Governments and trade unions, offered migrants far higher wages, with much less differentiation between skilled and unskilled men, than contemporary England. It was the setback of the Great Depression in the 1890s which led to the formation of strong trade unions, and also to the formation of the world's first Labour Governments. Out of this situation grew the establishment of arbitration courts, both Federal and State. Arbitration of wages and labor conditions is found hardly anywhere outside Australia and New Zealand. After some 60 or 70 years' experience, its value is now very much in doubt, but it appeals to the legalism of the Australian mind.

A written constitution became necessary for Australia in 1901, when six separate colonial governments federated to form a Commonwealth, which, however, was to possess only limited powers, the remainder being reserved for the component states. The Commonwealth Government, which is now in fact run by a powerful bureaucracy, with the political ministers playing only a minor part, is always seeking to extend its powers, principally by the underhand device of grabbing most of the revenue and handing it out as subsidies to the States. The Australian Constitution can be altered only by a referendum of the whole people, which must be carried, not just by a majority of the electors, but also in a majority of the component States.

As for Australian religion, education and culture, a remote and sparsely-populated country must inevitably live in a considerable degree of cultural dependence. Australia was originally dependent mainly upon Britain, but in recent years has been increasingly influenced by the United States. American influence is most marked in Sydney, the point at which it enters the system, and becomes less marked as you travel away from Sydney.

In contrast with New Zealand, which has remained rigidly British in outlook, Australia began to show signs of independent cultural development as early as the 1870s. It is a land which has produced some real poets, both in modern and in traditional styles. And there are few countries, other than Germany and Italy, where the appreciation of music is as widespread as it is in Australia. The Australian passions for sport and gambling are too well known to need reviewing.

25

White Australia

One-arm bandits in which
these Sydney, New South
Wales citizens delight are
illegal in the more straight-
laced other states.

26

Fingers of sea reach into
every quarter of Australia's
premier city, Sydney, just
north of Botany Bay, the
first settlement.

White collar men at the Holden Car Plant, Elizabeth, South Australia, improvise a bowls match in their lunch hour.

Workers from the General Motors assembly line at the Holden plant slump on the workroom floor to eat their packed lunches.

Religion has followed much the same trends as in other countries. The Australian population is about 25 per cent Catholic, representing not only those of Irish descent, but also a substantial number of Italian, Polish and Dutch descent. In the Protestant community, with its relatively large Scottish and Welsh elements, the Anglican Church does not have the predominance it has in England, and does not enjoy a special measure of State support and recognition. Australia is one of the few countries whose inhabitants are asked to declare their religion on the census form, though they are legally free to leave this question unanswered. Only a small proportion declare themselves irreligious, or leave the question unanswered.

Inadequate education of businessmen is largely responsible for low standards of business management, which in turn has led to the extensive takeover of Australian business by foreign interests. Recently there has been a large expansion of Australian universities, with somewhat questionable results. It is true that Australia's actual needs, from an economic point of view (as in many other countries) is not so much for additional universities as for additional Institutes of Advanced

Education, by whatever name they may be called, and for teaching courses similar to the Higher National Certificate in England.

The trouble is, as in England, that as fast as these institutions are founded they are breaking their necks to get themselves transformed into universities. The false prestige of the BA, and still more of the PhD, is now seen to be doing a great deal of economic and social harm. Primary education in Australia depends almost entirely on the State schools and the Catholic schools, with the latter gradually declining through shortage of teachers and money. There are virtually no other fee-charging primary schools.

But at the secondary school level the situation is entirely different. The Protestant Churches as well as the Catholic Church remain active in this field. The number of State High Schools is increasing; but they are generally believed not to give as good an education as the old established religious schools. It is touching to see the predicament of devout agnostics deciding whether to send their sons to church schools because they will get a better education there.

27

Farmers of the Australian outback

Australia has been called the Lucky Country, the Timeless Land, the Country of the Big Sky. But William Dampier, that gentlemanly buccaneer who made landfall on the north west coast in 1699, noted in his log-book that 'of all the places it has been my fortune to see, this is the most desolate and inhospitable.' Almost a century later Captain James Cook cast anchor at Botany Bay midway up the fertile eastern seaboard and pronounced it to be a suitable dumping ground for the overflow from George III's overcrowded jails. The events of the next two hundred years belong to the historians, what concerns us here is the effect this wide dichotomy in geographical and climatic conditions has had on the descendants of the 'first-footers' who were so unceremoniously flung into this outlandish place with no alternative other than to make the best of it, or perish. There were no half-measures, there was no way back. And this, perhaps, accounts for two of the most noteworthy Australian characteristics: the ability to stick things out and readiness to 'give it a go' regardless of the odds.

The Australian farmer's life can be unbelievably hard, yet he overcomes adversity, even drought, because of his tenacity and courage. The outback farmer everywhere shares the common hazards that threaten every man who wins his living from the land: those of fire and flood, drought and pestilence. No part of Australia is ever free of these, their effect is merely a matter of degree. Inland, the scourges are accepted as an inescapable factor of existence, while along the coast the rarity of their incursions lends them the awesome appearance of being a manifestation of divine displeasure.

The man along the coast lives cosily close to his neighbor, there are prosperous towns within easy distance of his front gate, he is in range of the local TV station, and the high tension wires of the State Electricity Commission spin their webs across the landscape. The man outback, however, may be a 100 miles or so from his nearest neighbor. A two-way radio is his chief contact with the outside world, and mail and papers come at irregular intervals, depending on whether the mail-plane is on schedule or an obliging passer-by calls in with the postbag. There are times when he sees no drop of rain from one year's end to another, others when the deluge comes, the dried-up rivers run a banker, and the red dust plains become a sea of sticky mud. He can then be marooned for weeks, as even the gallant little Cessnas or the DC 3s find it impossible to land on the rough and ready airstrip he has bulldozed out of the scrub.

His children while still young depend on the School of the Air which comes over the radio each morning from its base hundreds of miles away. Later, they are sent to complete their education in the cities and the homesteads grow painfully silent until school vacation brings them home again. If accident or illness strikes, an SOS will bring the Flying Doctor to his door, but at times the wait

29

'Home on the sheep' is an
Australian term indicating
success. Good grazing can
support an average of 3 sheep
to the acre; bad, only one to
20 acres.

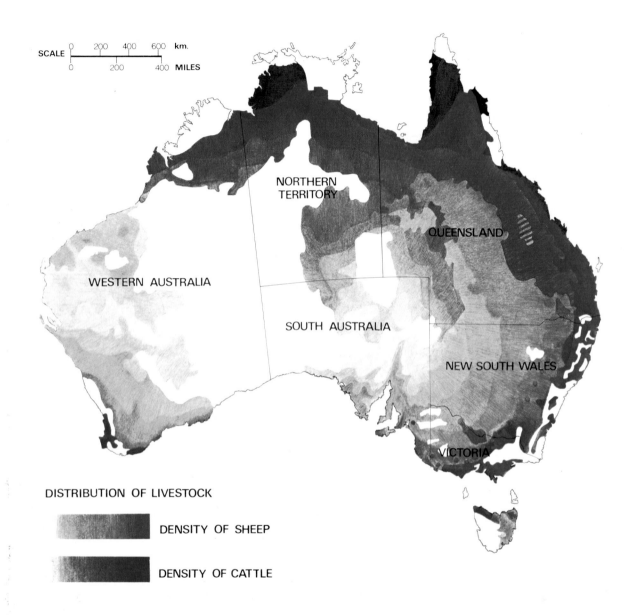

SCALE

DISTRIBUTION OF LIVESTOCK

DENSITY OF SHEEP

DENSITY OF CATTLE

NORTHERN TERRITORY

QUEENSLAND

WESTERN AUSTRALIA

SOUTH AUSTRALIA

NEW SOUTH WALES

VICTORIA

is agonizingly long, and if the 'wet' has closed the airstrip, it can be fatal.

The man along the fertile coastal areas can count on grazing two or even three sheep to the acre, a bullock-and-a-half to three, but 'up top-side' in the north and westwards on the far side of the Great Divide, a bullock to every square mile is the maximum he dare allow and still remain inside the margin of safety. If he grazes sheep, he may risk 20 to the square mile, that is every 640 acres. This accounts for the vast areas which these outback properties cover.

Some are the size of kingdoms, but the revenues yielded are as uncertain as the seasons and, apart from rare exceptions, few of them are liable for super tax.

The largest of them are no longer individually owned but have been taken over by the overseas investor. Alexandria Downs, the largest cattle-station in the world, 11,262 square miles in area, is a Vestey interest. Victoria River Downs, 5,494 square miles in area, belongs to another powerful business group. The King Ranch in Queensland is an American investment, off-shoot of its Texas namesake. There are also shrewd Australians whose acquaintance with the cattle country is limited to an examination of the map, who form companies and purchase leaseholds of the stations in the north, often when a protracted drought has ruined the men who

Lonely homesteads in the outback are sometimes built on stilts to offer shade from the intense summer heat — and protection from flooding.

There is no division of labor in the Never Never country. Station boss and station hand share equally in raising cattle under harsh conditions.

31

A drought can last for several years, leaving desolation in its wake. This disaster happens all too frequently in the arid north and center.

pioneered them 50 or 100 years ago. This in no way wins them popularity and they are referred to as the 'Collins House cattle kings.' Collins House, in Melbourne, being the nerve-center of much that is most influential in Australian financial affairs.

In the remote dry areas the sole source of water for the sheep and cattle are artesian bores which tap the subterranean rivers flowing far below the surface and pump the water up by means of diesel engines or enormous windmills. This means that the outback farmer must have a degree of mechanical skill as the failure of a pump can spell disaster if not rapidly repaired, and as professional mechanics are rarities; he must also have sufficient know-how to be able to mend the truck to get him there, should it break down.

Mustering and branding are two highlights in the outback farmer's year. Before the muster starts there is often a round up of wild horses, known as brumbies, which are then broken in to supplement the stock of station horses. These are particularly well suited to the bush because of their agility and stamina which are extremely important in view of the hazardous work they must perform.

It is in the great Red Center, where the sealed road ends, the bull-dust rises, and the homesteads thin, that one finds a separate kind of man and woman who have no counterpart elsewhere in Australia. Dead center in Australia lies the legendary town of Alice Springs which can only be reached by passing through a narrow gap in the Macdonnell Ranges. No other access is possible as the mountains stretch for long unbroken miles on either side and there is a belief that those who pass through Simpson's Gap fall victim to the spell of the Northern Territory and never wholly escape. This can be dismissed as 'Blackfeller talk,' but ask any of the hordes of tourists who run the gauntlet of the Gap each year and they will testify to a sensation of having left their personal problems on the other side, a lifting of the spirit and a sudden sense of freedom and release.

It should not be assumed from this that either Shangri La or El Dorado wait on the far side of the Gap. The Territory is both tough and uncompromising. To come to terms with it requires a special kind of courage, a tenacity of purpose and ability to endure that is undreamed of in the south. Nevertheless there *is* a kind of magic there, otherwise what brings the tourists back again and again, many of them to stay? The Territory is unbelievably beautiful. It is perhaps best seen by air as the roads are for the most part rough and dusty, the exception being the Stuart Highway which runs 1,000 dead straight miles between Alice Springs and Darwin, the only towns of any size in the entire 523,262 square miles – an area the size of Ohio, Indiana, Illinois, Michigan and Wisconsin combined.

Seen from the air the brilliant colors and the vastness of the Territory become apparent, with the isolated

station homesteads looking like ships becalmed in an ocean of red earth. Should the plane carry mail, great activity will be observed as it circles round the cluster of iron roofs and a truck will come hurrying out to meet it as it lands. The 'boss,' his wife, the kids, and a miscellaneous collection of station blacks and skinny dogs will come tumbling out. It is unbelievable how many can pack into the ubiquitous 'ute' – short for utility – the sturdy truck that serves so many purposes.

Thermoses of scalding tea, cakes and buttered scones – baking powder biscuit – will be produced and consumed in the shade of a wing, while the *lubras* – Aboriginal women – and the piccanninies hover round and wait for the mail to be unloaded. And not only mail. Cases of beer, tinned food, spare parts for an engine, extra tires, knitting wool, much needed medicine, feeding-bottles for a baby, seed potatoes, day old chicks – the mailman will deliver almost anything. The requests have been made via the radio network centered at the Flying Doctor Base, which not only answers calls for help but relays messages of every conceivable variety.

The men of the Center seem to measure up to the preconceived idea of what a Territorian should be. Lean and suntanned, they are given to few words, and their eyes are accustomed to great distances and to squinting at the sun. They also have an uncanny knack of assessing the worth of a stranger and, should he fail to measure up to standards, can be ruthless in their rejection of him. Isolation does not seem to trouble the women, there are few neurotics and the marriages seem exceptionally sound.

On rare occasions they will visit Alice Springs or Darwin, an annual visit to the sea is not unknown, provided that the season has been good, and it is safe to say that for the women of the outback boredom is an evil that is practically unknown – they have far too much to do. There is cooking and the supervision of the children's school-work, sewing and a good deal of the housework, as the *lubras* are a doubtful asset when it comes to sharing the domestic chores.

When her man is absent, as he frequently must be, the outback farmer's wife will assume command with an efficiency that is equal to his own. The absences are rarer than they used to be. The advent of the road-train with its chain of double-decker cages, capable of transporting several hundred head of cattle at a time, has largely done away with the long droves overland which could last weeks or even months. But not entirely. The old stock routes still reverberate to the passing of a thousand head of 'beef on the hoof' on its way to Wyndham, Darwin, or the railhead at Alice Springs.

It is part of the tradition of the north that the families of the native stockmen, without whom no cattleman could survive, should stay with him. They build their camps close to the homestead and live in happy idleness in *wurlies* – tumble-down bark shelters – along with uncles, aunts and grandfathers, and an astonishing collection of

scraggy dogs. They draw rations from the station store-room, lining up for pills, and ointment for sore eyes; advice on how to cure a baby who has colic, not forgetting iodine and sticking plaster for split lips and lacerated scalps, these last generally the penalty for tangled love-affairs. All such jobs are routine for the station-owner's wife, which she discharges with good-humor, skill and great forbearance.

For recreation they have books and the daily gossip with distant neighbors over the two-way radio, known as the 'galah session,' so-called because of the chatter that takes place between the pretty rosy-colored parrots of that name. And, of course, the annual races, high-spot in the social calendar which are held on one of the larger stations, a three-day fiesta at which friends, both black and white, forgather from a distance of anything from 100 to 500 miles. The races are run with scant regard to the rules laid down by the Jockey Club and what the horses lack in pedigree they make up in enthusiasm. The nights are enlivened with dancing and much drinking, with the colored patrons holding their own *corrobboree* – Aboriginal festivity – a mile or so away. When it is over, cars and trucks and semi-trailers start on the long drive homewards, disappearing in great clouds of dust. All that remains are the empty beer-cans, bottles, and the recollection of three memorable days. But most are not sorry to return to the lonely outback.

33

John Macarthur introduced
the profitable Merino sheep
to Australia in 1803. Despite
a decline, wool remains a
staple industry.

Small Town Australians

The time-suspended town lies cradled in the valley, its main street flanked with the timber-pillared verandahs of yesteryear; there is a hitching rail in its center in front of a coaching inn. The court house, jail and post office are convict-built. The facing rows of buildings are turn of the century stage sets, silver corrugated roofs, white and pastel facades, beige and mango bricks. Iron hatted cottages flow from the center into the hills above the river, a lusty winter tributary, which, come summer, dries to a string of somber pools. A 3,000 foot mountain casts its reflection on the tree-fringed river. Twenty years ago about 4,000 people lived in and around this typical Australian town. Now the population has dwindled to 2,000.

I remembered swimming in the river and wading up the creeks that ran into it; catching leeches, tadpoles, frogs and yabbies – a delicious fresh-water crustacean. Those were the days of endless picnics about the country streams during the all-too-brief autumn. They were followed by a hunt for the elusive seasonal mushrooms, a rare item which lured the city and beach people to the bush. In the equally fleeting springtime, the picnics were followed by a search for wildflowers; orchids, kangaroo paws and many other eccentric blossoms that grew from a landface as old as time. All these outings were accompanied by their incumbent pests; flies, mosquitoes and ants; one ant always managed to flavor someone's sandwich with the pungent and revolting tang of formic acid. We rode frequently as children out to the foot of the mountain to the Mile Poole, where there were Chinese market gardens. At the foot of the other hill was an apiary, owned by a boozy band of Irish brothers who robbed honey from the bees that fed on the delicately scented eucalyptus blossoms. Up the hill at the side of the mountain there were wheatfields and grazing sheep that belonged to descendants of one of the first settlers.

We attended the Protestant State School but were sent to a nearby convent for music lessons from the nuns. There was an occasional invasion of Aborigine children at the state school which usually lasted about three weeks. They vanished as suddenly as they came – gone walkabout. When the holidays came we were sent as were most farmers' children after harvest to beach resorts, to escape the apathy of the long hot summer.

Twenty years later there was little change. Honey was still available. The locals swam in a freshwater pool of Olympic proportions. School children still went to the sea in summer and the all-too-few remaining wildflowers were protected. The Chinese had gone from the Mile Poole and so had their gardens but Albanians cultivated vegetable and melon crops over by the cemetery. There were Italians with a citrus orchard who were not doing so well as the climate was too hot. The kindergarten teacher, who had suffered the town's children for three generations, had gone back to Killarney – or to Heaven.

34   The cream and green café, which doled out pies, ices

In every small town there is a local cricket team which regularly plays with teams from neighboring towns.

Aborigines sit outside their caravan in Coober Pedy. They get money by 'fossicking' — picking up opal chips.

A tough life in a harsh climate shows on the face of a typical Coober Pedy opal miner, smoking a 'roll your own.'

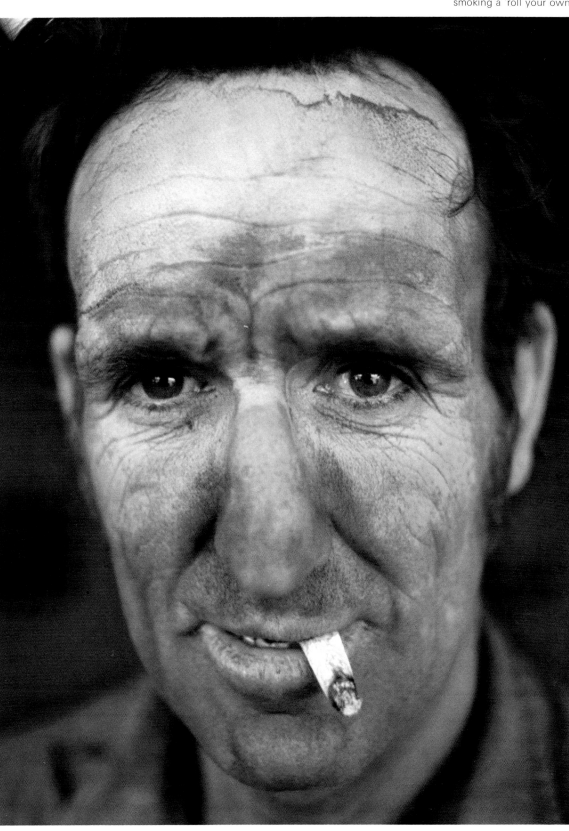

Small Town Australians

An unshaven miner quenches his thirst, born of a hot, dusty day's work in Coober Pedy. He swiftly downs six beers in half-pint measures called schooners.

(Opposite) Hill End in NSW was a thriving 'gold rush' town in the 1860s. Now its population numbers a couple of hundred. Local residents still gather at the pub.

and overdone eggs on overdone steaks duly smothered in 'black' or tomato sauce, was still run by Greeks. So too the fish and chip shop which still sold baby shark as snapper. Both did a roaring trade from the truckies, big paunchy men with red rimmed eyes in the uniform of all Australian laborers; a faded indigo singlet, black football shorts and boots or thong sandals. An Italian now ran the greengrocer's shop. The pharmacy had been taken over by one of the chemist's sons; the other now ran the news agency. The old Doctor, by virtue of his calling, the town's senior citizen, had retired. His place had been taken by a 'city slicker' and the old, convict-built hospital had been supplanted by a modern one near the equally new high-school.

Most of the community (for everyone owns a car) goes 20 miles to a larger town to shop in supermarkets or to the city, where you can buy 'anything you can get anywhere else in the whole world.' The owner of the oldest hotel, a descendant of a Scots family, had handed the license to his youngest son and retired to the city. The first-born son had built a lavishly furnished delusion of grandeur in the bush. His wife, a girl who had money from meat, had taken cookery lessons abroad and, having polished up her vowels at the same time, now rated the self-designated job of hostess to visiting minor celebrities. There was a permanently pinned thank-you note from Godfrey Winn on a cork board in the 'lounge.' The open air cinema gardens of the old town hall, where the films were invisible until the light suddenly fell, and whose sound effects could be heard all over the town, had

been abandoned in favor of a drive-in a mile out; a passion pit for youth to play courting games with little encouragement from the movies. The Commonwealth censor, to control their ardor, cut a minute from *Camelot*. The grocer's shop remained in the hands of the once German family who had settled during the Gold Rush.

'The old family,' who once lived in the huge verandahed bungalow that gazed over the whole valley, was no longer there. The father, a stout squire of English stock who had made country racing a smart city pastime, was dead and his widow had gone east to join her grandchildren and a daughter who had once been considered a great beauty in English court circles. All that remained of a fantastic terraced garden were a few straggly rose bushes, the pungent frangipani which grows everywhere like a weed, a tangled mass of bougainvillea, and the hanging baskets of aspidistras and maidenhair fern. The house had been acquired by a local starting-price bookie and the land had been broken up and added to other farms. Bank managers, portly and affluent, were treated with awe by the locals, possibly because they held all the farm mortgages.

The descendants of the early settlers still farmed the hillside, but now lived in the town on 'nob hill.' Here, successful retired farmers built creamy brick mansions with porches – the doors with decorative iron outer screens facing onto the fly wire. Their mantelpieces were invariably littered with family snaps, and plaster ducks floating up textured walls. The strip of front lawn with a surrounding border of hardy flowers was in constant use for barbecues, usually hosted by the eldest sons. Noticeably absent were younger sons and daughters who were either at 'College' in the city or had taken jobs there. In the main, the town was composed of Anglo-Saxon stock and their offspring still intermarry.

Three miles along the southern road were the decaying wurlies – Aborigine shacks, rotting car parts and bony kangaroo dogs surrounding a life of abject squalor made possible by government relief. The ragged inhabitants still make an occasional sortie into town, usually ending in a sweet sherry spree on Sunday nights; their fights leading to clashes with the Salvation Army, who come out loud and clear on this one night.

For such a small community there were a vast string of clubs. The Junior Farmers, a good-natured wild bunch who drove their dirty 'utes' – utility trucks – at great speed, worked hard and played harder. There was the Apex Rotary and Lions, all do-gooder clubs, the ever powerful Returned Soldiers League and its associate Legacy, who look after war widows and their children, and the secretive Masons, creeping off to Lodge. Of the church societies the Catholic headed by a 'Mick' priest was the mightiest and the Methodist the most anonymous; as non-drinkers they were not quite 'in,' in a town where all social life revolves around the pubs.

Ladies of all churches backed the Country Woman's Association which put up preserves at Church fêtes,

Small Town Australians

The owner, Mrs Brewster, sits
outside the Coober Pedy
garage and general store,
which sells everything from
gelignite to frozen peas.

The single rail track, seen here
as it approaches Kingoonya,
the nearest stop to Coober
Pedy, runs 1,000 miles from
Adelaide to Alice Springs.

Coober Pedy is the Aboriginal name for White Man's Hole in the Ground. Here the population lives underground to escape the burning heat.

served the teas at the never ending race meetings and threw a lunch party annually for the visiting Miss Australia. There were cricket and Australian Rules Football clubs, seasonal efforts which challenge and visit nearby towns. Bowling clubs (adjoining the tennis club), have become a white-uniformed craze among the over-sixties. Smartest of them all was the golf club; it had its own bar and often gave elegant tea parties.

A small town wedding is an epic-sized event. First there is the bachelor party; the buck show with its over-tones of sacrifice, for the groom is giving up his highly prized freedom, his all. What sexual experience he has may have been with the fiancée or it may have been gained from the town 'bike,' the generous girl of easy virtue who gave her favors in the back of the 'ute.' All mates gather together, make lots of ribald jokes then aim to get both the groom and themselves paralytically drunk. Practical jokes may involve stripping the groom, tying him to a tree and blackening him with boot polish – one unfortunate was thus delivered trussed-up on his fiancée's doorstep. Another was sent from Perth to Melbourne on a one-way ticket only three days before his wedding.

The bride-to-be has a kitchen tea where she is given 'plastic' utensils, and shows off her trousseau which has been purchased in the city with a bridesmaid and mother. Mother will wear a matching ensemble in see-through organza or Thai silk and her hat will be dome-shaped with guipure lace around the brim. The men are poured into their one suit which they wear with as much grace as a hair shirt. There will be 200 guests at the reception – either out of doors or in the Town Hall – who will eat curry and rice, cold ham and chicken, then fruit salad and ice-cream. Beer and sparkling sweet wine will be drunk and 'a good time was had by all' will be the report in the local gazette.

In a different way the mining town depends on the vagaries of Mother Earth. It is here today (Coober Pedy) gone tomorrow (Hill End). It is a curiosity. But in the typical Australian town there is a sameness in all things. The leaves, the sky and the people are near the color of the earth, and there is a khaki similarity in their dress, an evenness in speech, a conformity that runs as far as the unseasoned food and its lack of variety.

Here the light is so bright it bleaches out all color, turns eyes to squinting slits, skin to leather and withers the young to middle age in their early thirties. It is an earthy and salty community, where women have been known to tell rude stories and the men drop their Hs and Gs. 'We don't mindem, we don't likem' – they mean dagoes (southern Europeans), wogs (colored Asians), wowsers (teetotallers) or boongs (Aborigines).

An English migrant complaining of the heat, the dust and the flies had a terse reply: 'this is a hard country – there's nothing softer here.' 'No,' she snapped, 'only the wool!'

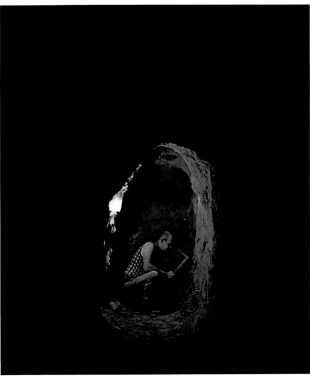

39

An opal-mine shaft in Coober Pedy is sometimes sunk 120 feet in the hills but opal can be found at 20 feet on the flat.

Northern Aborigines
Australia

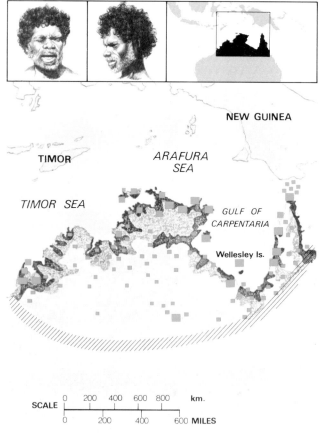

NEW GUINEA

TIMOR

ARAFURA
SEA

TIMOR SEA

GULF OF
CARPENTARIA

Wellesley Is.

SCALE
0 200 400 600 800 km.
0 200 400 600 MILES

Aboriginal settlements

Traditionally the Australian Aborigines were hunters and gatherers. There is a basic similarity in their manner of gaining a living which tempts people to think of the tribes as being the same with only minor variations. We do not encounter such striking differences in Australia as we do among African societies. Instead the differences are more subtle and, as in the marriage system, neither readily seen nor easily understood.

Although the northern tribes came into contact with outsiders before the southern tribes, many of them have managed to survive and retain something of their social organization and systems of thought. The coastal tribes of Arnhem Land, for instance, came into contact with Malayan/Indonesian fishermen probably centuries before the arrival of the British. These fishermen arrived by the north-west monsoons, and sought out the abundant bêche-de-mer fishing grounds. They stayed some months and hired Aboriginal labor until they caught the seasonal south-east winds home. In the northern part of Cape York Peninsula, in Queensland, the Aborigines came into contact with a different outside influence, the Torres Strait Islanders and, through them, the New Guinea cultures.

41

The sacred rocks of Elcho
Island form a vantage point for
the Aborigines. Their bodies
are painted in clay, a
decoration for dances and
initiation ceremonies.

A Djingaloo Aborigine completes a cave painting on Wessel Island. It records an episode of the tribe's dreamtime history.

The Lardil, who inhabit Mornington Island, in the Gulf of Carpentaria, Northern Queensland, possess rich food resources. Water can be easily obtained in many places along the island's beaches. Traditionally there were a number of main camping places which were used for long periods so that one could reasonably describe the Lardil as being semi-sedentary. They could hunt during the day and return to the camp at night.

In the past the Lardil were fairly isolated but they managed to visit the neighboring islands on rafts made out of light mangrove wood. On rare occasions, such as when a young man was to be initiated, they would even visit the mainland tribes. But the rafts could only be used in calm weather for they were unsafe in rough seas and sudden squalls could easily capsize them.

From the land they gather many kinds of roots, berries, yams, panjas, and water lilies, and they hunt wallabies, swamp turtles, ducks, geese, lizards and goannas. From the sea they obtain many different kinds of fish such as mullet, salmon, rock cod and barramundi, all of which they catch in rock traps and nets, or by hooks, lines and spears. Probably the most important foods are sea

(Above) An Arnhem Land Aborigine strips a tree of its bark, to be used later for highly colored paintings, stretched like canvas over a simple frame.

The huge thumbnail of the Aborigine is used both as a weapon and a tool. Fish are swiftly gutted and even small animals killed without resort to other implements.

An Aborigine of Elcho Island carefully works on a bark painting of a tribal dance. Dyes for the colors come from clays, natural iron oxides and charcoal.

The map indicates the areas of
pure blood (mauve) or mixed
blood (green) aborigines — and
where most are to be found
(blue squares).

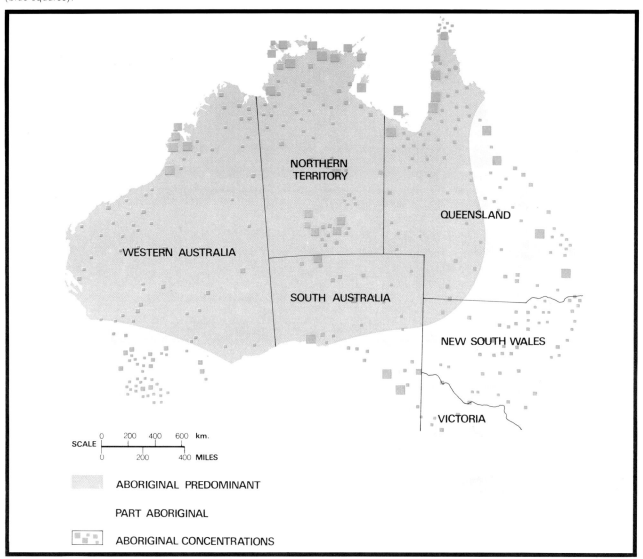

NORTHERN
TERRITORY

QUEENSLAND

WESTERN AUSTRALIA

SOUTH AUSTRALIA

NEW SOUTH WALES

VICTORIA

SCALE
0 200 400 600 km.
0 200 400 MILES

ABORIGINAL PREDOMINANT

PART ABORIGINAL

ABORIGINAL CONCENTRATIONS

turtles and dugongs. The large sea turtles crawl up the sandy beaches to dig their nests and lay their eggs. During the egg-laying season the females can easily be rendered helpless by turning them over on their backs. The nests are soon found by the Aborigines who follow the huge tracks made by the turtle as she struggles up the beach on her flippers. Often more than 100 eggs are to be found buried in the sand.

The area is a special feeding and breeding ground for dugongs, or sea cows. Dugongs are aquatic mammals and weigh several hundred pounds. These mammals have become so completely adapted to the sea that they even give birth in the water. The Lardil say that a pregnant female about to give birth is sometimes chased by a shark, but she outwits it by coming close to shore and swirling the mud. She then gives birth in the murky water.

Traditionally the Lardil catch dugongs in strong rope nets when they come up the larger rivers to feed on the lush aquatic plants. The nets are strung out in the middle of the river at low tide and bushes are arranged along the sides so as to form a sort of corral. One man stands at the mouth of the river to signal to the others when a dugong starts swimming up the river. At night he has a torch made out of paper bark with which to signal. Men on rafts patrol the sides of the river; their job is to get behind the dugong so as to block off its retreat and, by yelling and hitting the water, they try to frighten it so that it panics and rushes into the nets. A couple of men stand near the net and poke the dugong along with their spears.

This is a dangerous moment, for the dugong might rush at one of the net holders and so break his limbs and entangle him in the net. This is rare, however, and usually the dugong is caught in the net and quickly rendered helpless by the tail end being picked out of the water. All the power of a dugong is in the tail—the flippers are mainly used for steering – so that once the 43 tail is out of the water there is little that it can do. After this it is rolled up the beach, or as the Lardil language so picturesquely expresses it, 'The dugong is caused to rise to the beach.'

The meat is shared under strict and complex rules and, when we examine this distribution, we can see how it symbolizes the structure of Lardil society. Just as they recognize different age categories among themselves so also do they recognize different categories of dugongs, *viz.*, boss dugong, old man dugong, young man dugong, old woman dugong, pregnant dugong, baby dugong. The piece of meat one receives depends on a number of factors, such as the kind of dugong caught, where it was caught, who was present and what part one played in catching it. With a large dugong, owners of the 'country' where it was caught have rights to the meat from the tail, chest, flippers and back of the neck. But if it is a small dugong then those whose mother came from the 'country' have sole right to these pieces of meat.

The Lardil are divided into some 30 odd patriclans. Each clan owns a small stretch of land, called their country, with unrestricted access and rights to the sea directly in front. These countries are very small. They have a coastline of not more than five miles and the bush land seldom extends inland for more than a few miles. Nor are the clans very large for they seldom number more than 15 or 20 people. The Lardil say that the land belongs to all the members of the tribe so that people have a right to travel and to hunt in the country of other clans. Nevertheless the owners of the country, even if they are not present, have certain rights to any food caught in their country. If a large fish is speared in a fish trap in another man's country, the fish must be cut in half so that an equal share can be given to the *dulmadas*. When the water-lily season approaches after the rains, it is the

Aborigine women attempt to entice the initiates away from the forthcoming circumcision ritual. They are testing manhood and courage.

These long cone-shaped dancing hats are made from bark, tied together with human hair. They are worn at the end of the circumcision ceremony.

The initiation of boys involves painful rituals. Here circumcision is carried out — nowadays with old razor blades, up to recently with stone knives.

owners of the country in which the swamp lies who direct the gathering. People from the northern part of the island pick lilies from the northern part, and so on. The owners of the country have the right to pick lilies only from the center. This kind of geographical organization is the basis of all rights.

Yet the Lardil rarely stay in their clan-country for it is normally too small to support all its members. In each cardinal point of the island there is a main camping place where the Aborigines spend most of their time. On rare occasions, especially during the *dulnhu* season, all the members of the tribe would gather together in one place. The *dulnhu* season comes in October when schools of the *dulnhu* fish swim around the island in a clockwise direction. The abundance of these fish can support the whole population for many weeks. But there are too many taboos surrounding the catching, cooking and eating of the *dulnhu*. At the time of the new moon, all spears must point to the ground, so that the moon will not be reminded that in mythical times he was killed because of his greed. It is also forbidden to spear the fish. They may only be caught in nets and cooked in a special fire made out of tea-tree wood.

It is difficult to understand the complex thought that governs the Aborigine's concept of time. A general pattern among most tribes is that there is *here* and *now* which every person experiences – and running parallel to this is *dreamtime* which people slip into while they are asleep. In the distant past, the Aborigines believe, there was only *dreamtime*, but somehow, at some point, there was a split – and the difference between waking and sleeping time emerged. For this reason the strange things that happen in dreams have, in fact, some reality. *Dreamtime* is like another world and however this may be, the Lardil realize that only a few gifted people ever experience the joy of hearing the spirits of *dreamtime* singing to them. But from these songs, heard in sleep, come most of the dances that make up another important part of Lardil culture.

The Lardil are renowned for their dancing. They claim that the spirits of the underworld, or dreamtime spirits, come to them in their sleep so that a dreamer can hear them singing and sometimes he can even see them dancing. At times one can hear men singing in their sleep and it is believed that this is the dreamtime people singing. Those who are present may take up the song and practise it so that it will not be lost, or else the dreamer himself may wake up, and start singing it over and over again so that he will not forget it.

The dances play an important part in Lardil competitive displays, for besides being divided into a number of clans they are also divided into two main groups, the northerners and southerners, or as they are more usually called, the windward and leeward people. There is much conflict between these two groups which at times breaks out in fierce fighting. It is also given expression in the dances. 45

During a phase of the circumcision ceremony the boys are laid upon their fathers to symbolize filial ties which will soon be broken.

Each of the two groups have their own dancing ground where they practise their latest dances. They keep their new dances secret until they are ready to show them at a common dancing ground. Although to the outsider the differences may be negligible, both sides make acid comments about the other's singing and dancing.

The dances are often about animals and birds, such as native companion, eagle hawks, wallabies and honey bees, and things that have happened to them. It may describe a hunter alone in the bush who hears a bird singing to him, and which gradually leads him away deeper into the bush so that he becomes lost. Or else it may imitate the search for honey – in Australia the indigenous bees do not sting – or the gathering of water lilies. But sometimes it is a big dance; about one of the mythical beings such as the Rainbow Serpent who was burnt to death in dreamtime.

The dancer's paraphernalia includes a hair belt, a dancing hat and bundles of leaves. The rustling of the leaves suggests wind. The dancing hat is cone shaped, and it is made out of bark which is tied together with human hair which has been rolled so as to form string. Two or three emu feathers adorn the top. These feathers are much sought after, but as emus are not found on Mornington Island nor on any of the neighboring islands, the Lardil have to trade for them with the mainland tribes. Usually they give boomerangs in return. Some men also wear a white band around their forehead if they have passed through both stages of initiation. Hanging down on each side are wallaby teeth. These represent dog teeth, for dog teeth are considered to be too powerful to wear, since in dreamtime a dog also went through the first initiation.

Like almost all the Aboriginal tribes of Australia the Lardil have to contend with the onrush of 'civilization.' The complexity and power of an industrialized society has brought much uncertainty and puzzlement to these people who have before known only the very simplest of lives. They find themselves attracted by the material goods of the European, the axes and knives, blankets and whiskey. Some of these things make life easier, others relieve the boredom that an easier life brings. Yet few of the Aborigines are attracted by the society that the new Australians offer.

In reviewing the history of Aborigine contact with the whites, it is conspicuous that both the first and permanent contacts are made with frontiersmen. It is a sad fact that many of these white men of the outback are less concerned than they might be in the preservation of Aboriginal culture. Too often no attempt is made to understand the ways of the Aborigine and without an appreciation of primitive cultures, little progress can be made in assimilating those people into a modern world.

The Lardil, like other Australian Aborigines, have a highly complex system of marriage. Yet in contrast, the marriage system of the whites seems strangely uncomplicated. White men appear to marry just anybody,

An Aborigine family is on the move in typical Arnhem Land scrub. The dog is merely a scavenging companion – but will warn of danger at night.

Goannas form an important
part of the Aborigine diet. The
Aborigines are adept at
catching even the smallest and
quickest reptiles.

Lardil Aborigines roll a dead
dugong — aquatic mammal —
onto the beach, before
dividing the flesh by strict
tribal rules.

unlike the Lardil whose marriage partners strictly con-
form to social customs and taboos. In this matter the
Lardil consider the whites no better than animals who
mate without discrimination. This quickly illustrates the
confusion, bordering on contempt, that so easily arises
from misunderstanding.

Nevertheless it is the white Australians who have the
power. Relentlessly the values and social systems of the
Aborigines are being eroded – and despite the Government's policy of assimilation, too many of those in
continuous contact with Aborigines have very different
attitudes. The few missionaries and dedicated anthropologists can hardly do enough to redress the balance.

A small child eats a lizard
after it has been roasted. Its
grease, often rubbed into the
skin, is thought to have great
healing properties.

A Northern Aborigine who has
speared a wallaby returns to
share it with his encampment.
It will be buried in live coals
for even roasting.

Gibson Desert Aborigines
Australia

At the Waleluka claypan near
Pulykara rainfall is erratic.
Aborigines can go waterless
longer than Europeans:
they consequently drink more
at a time.

Only 3,000 Aborigines inhabit the Gibson Desert, the size of Arizona. At Pulykara, Aborigines saw their first white man in 1969.

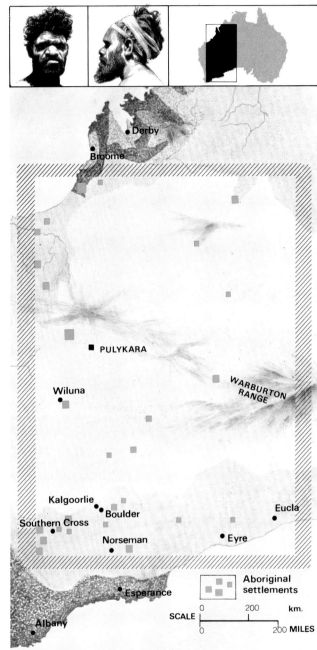

Derby

Broome

PULYKARA

Wiluna

WARBURTON RANGE

Kalgoorlie

Boulder

Southern Cross

Eucla

Norseman

Eyre

Esperance

Albany

Aboriginal settlements

SCALE

0 200 km.

0 200 MILES

I t is hunting time in the Gibson Desert in the hot, dusty and fly-ridden outback of Australia. Two men with spears lie in wait in a circular brush blind not far from the camp where, with other members of their tribe, they have made a halt in their wanderings through the harsh spinifex grass of the desert. Their target now is emu, the bird that looks like a big feather duster on legs and can run at 30 miles an hour. Their lure is a water soakhole they have dug a few yards from the blind.

49

The hours pass slowly. The only shade to protect the hunters comes from a small mulga tree. Their only entertainment while they wait is the chewing of plugs of tobacco. Then . . . a booming note. An emu is approaching and the hunters attach their spears to the holders which they use to propel the weapons. There will be a chance for only one shot. The emu nears. When it is only 30 feet away, the spear flies through the air. Missed! The bird has fled.

There will be no more emu found this day but there is compensation on the way back to the camp. Much of the protein in the diet of these desert Aborigines comes from lizards, which exceed mammal life in these harsh, inhospitable areas. The hunters find the tracks of one. After ten minutes of tracking through the clumps of desert grass, they find the lizard's hole and stamp on the ground above to trap it in its tunnel. One hunter grabs a stick and uses it to dig. Only a foot underground, there is the lizard – a type of goanna weighing a little over three pounds. Small enough but something to take back to supplement the grubs, termites and the plant foods that the women of the tribe will have been searching for.

With the women go the children and the dogs. Although the dun-coloured dingo dogs introduced to Australia by man 3,000 years ago, run wild in packs, the Aborigine keeps many as pets. So, as the women stride forward, carrying bowls of water to refresh themselves, the children and dogs run around and ahead of them pursuing small lizards which scurry about to avoid the voracious jaws. It is a good day for foraging. First there are clumps of ripe *ngaru* and other fruit. *Ngaru* look like small green tomatoes and are a staple food of the desert people. Only the outer husk is eaten and this is deftly split from the seeds with a sharp flat stick which the women carry in their hair. *Kampurarpa*, a fruit of similar appearance, fortunately ripens in the opposite season to *Ngaru*, providing the Aborigine with year round nutrition. There is plenty to be picked and three large wooden bowls are filled in less than an hour – about 30 pounds of fruit. So the scorching walk back to the camp can begin.

The Gibson Desert Aborigines are an astonishing remnant of a primitive way of life. Many of them live near the Woomera rocket range but many still use stone tools of man's earliest pattern while Whitefella is busy putting new stars in the sky. Archaeological research has shown that man has been in Australia for at least 20,000 years and that at all times the manner of living was by hunting and foraging for food. No evidence has been found that agriculture was ever developed until white men discovered and developed the continent. The only industry seems to have been the making of stone tools, usually held in the hand but sometimes hafted. Even today, although steel axes and knives are eagerly sought and coveted, more remote Aborigines still make their own stone tools.

Many Aborigines have massive brow ridges, which reminded earlier researchers of Neanderthal man. Later studies confirm the view of the American anthropologist Sherwood L. Washburn that 'the Aboriginal Australian is definitely a modern man and lacks the peculiarities of the face and limb bone which characterize ancient man.' The Aboriginal skin is dark, their noses are broad, body hair plentiful and their limbs are slender. They have become highly adapted to the harsh conditions of desert life: strong teeth and jaw muscles to cope with the raw or almost raw food that they eat, thickly calloused soles of the feet to cope with walking barefoot over the sharp stones and thorns of the desert. A man can walk for hours with small thorns stuck in the bottom of his feet, picking them out only at the end of his journey.

The language of the Western Desert Aborigines is largely Pitjantjara, but there is a web of interchangeable dialect, and members of one tribe will frequently use the speech of others he may be visiting as a sign of respect. The total population of Western Desert Aborigines is estimated at about 3,000. This is a rough estimate because the tribes wander over an area the size of the State of New Mexico. They will travel many miles both in search of food and to visit neighbors. It is likely that even at the time of the first contact with Europeans, the Aboriginal population in the desert was low. The evidence indicates that the Aborigines have lived in isolation for thousands of years but have maintained enough contact among themselves to keep their dialects mutually intelligible.

The American anthropologist Professor Richard A. Gould of the University of Hawaii recently visited a small group of Aborigines who were said never to have met Europeans. Ironically, they had been tracked down in late 1969 by a patrol officer from the Weapons Research Establishment at Woomera. Professor Gould found them, after an arduous journey by cross-country vehicle, in the heart of the Gibson Desert at a place called Pulykara. Their camp consisted of three small clusters of hearths each surrounded by clear patches of sand (sleeping and sitting areas) and these were protected by a low brush windbreak. Burned acacia trees and low shrubs surrounded the camp and there was a waterhole to the southwest. The people were timid but typical of Aboriginals untouched by Western civilization in living entirely by hunting and foraging on land that in terms of food resources is probably the poorest in the world. The men hunted regularly for emu, kangaroos and other game but it was the women who provided most of the diet, gathering berries and fruits such as quandongs, and seeds as well as lizards and other small game.

Because of their wandering way of life, travelling from one waterhole to the next, running game before them and always in search of the plants next to ripen, the Aborigines have a portable material existence. They take with them spears, clubs, wooden bowls and digging and throwing sticks, much of this equipment being carried in string belts which are made from human hair. Tools often

An Aborigine woman carries a young dingo round her waist near Pulykara. She sympathetically covers its eyes so it will not see her eat.

At Mulangiri the wandering Aborigines seek some shade at their camp. Even here the temperature may reach 118°F in the summer.

Smoke signals are the only way to tell fellow tribesmen of the discovery of wild foodstuff. This man lights a signal fire of spinifex grass near Pulykara.

A fire provides warmth during the cold desert nights and cooked food for a lone Aboriginal woman in a winter camp near Pulykara.

Gibson Desert Aborigines Australia

A lone hunter returns from a
successful day on the sandhills
near Pulykara. The wild-cat he
has killed will feed the whole
camp.

Grubs are speared on a stick
for easy carrying. They
provide an everyday food
supplement for the Desert
Aborigines.

Quandongs (*Santalum Acumi-
natum*) have been collected
near Pulykara. The succulent
outer coat provides a
valuable source of nutrition.

A Nyatunyatjara-dialect
speaking Aborigine woman
winnows *wanguna* seeds.
Women prepare food while
men hunt.

have more than one use and this is particularly true of the spear thrower, of which the desert Aborigines are the last people in the world to make extensive use. The thrower gives extra leverage to the cast of the spear and, with long practice, it is possible to hurl the weapon as far as 100 yards. The spear thrower is also used as a friction stick in firemaking and as a drum, which is tapped during some religious ceremonies. Often the thrower is incised with elaborate patterns as also are the boards used in ritual ceremonies.

Decoration plays an important part in Aboriginal ritual. The sacred boards, which are hidden in the scrub when not in use, are very elaborate, as are the bullroarers which are used to scare away women and uninitiated men when a ceremony is taking place. Patterns similar to those on the boards are painted on men's bodies during rituals. The rock paintings which are found in many places in Aborigine territory are usually of the same kind of geometric patterns, as though acting as a reminder through history to the next generations of practitioners in the ritual.

The complex root of Aboriginal faith is 'dreamtime', a timeless age before the historic past but continuing now. In the dreamtime totemic beings, such as the possum, the kangaroo and the water snake, travelled across the desert leaving their influence in sacred places, still to influence the lives of people of today. The tracks taken by the dreamtime beings cross and recross in a web over the desert.

Australian Aboriginal society is divided into cult-lodges, consisting of men who believe themselves to be descended in the male line from the same dreamtime being. Women may belong to these lodges but their ceremonies may only be carried out by men. The most significant of these ceremonies is circumcision, which for the more fortunate is preceded by a grand tour of distant camps where the novice is shown sacred dances and taught sacred songs. Before the ceremony, the novices are kept in seclusion, their food being brought to them from the camp. During this time, which may last five weeks, they are taught the sacred songs, which tell of the adventures of the dreamtime beings. During the waiting time, the older men of the camp sing continually and perform dances, which are short but require hours of preparation in decorating the body in sacred traditional patterns with ash and clay.

At dawn on the day of the circumcision ceremony, the women sit apart while the men sing the songs of the dreamtime Kangaroo while the novices lie concealed under blankets. More dances, and then ocher and charcoal pigments are applied to the dancers' bodies while blood from the arm is sprinkled over them. At sunset, it is time for the climax of the ceremony. Enormous bonfires are lit and the naked novices are brought out, some of the older men forming a table with their backs while the operation is performed.

Circumcision and the silent acceptance of pain are the beginning of Aboriginal man's further tuition in the ritual practices of his cult-lodge. Professor A. P. Elkin wrote: 'It is almost impossible for those who have not witnessed such ceremonies to realize the important part they play in strengthening the unity and sense of common purpose in the tribe as a whole.'

The Aboriginal takes more than one wife, even in the settlements and missions where so many of them now live. It is in these places that the impact of Westernized society on primitive man is most seen. They live in rough corrugated iron shacks. Some work in mining, others on menial tasks such as chopping firewood, carving touristic boomerangs and making sun-dried bricks.

Nakedness does not worry the desert Aboriginal but in the settlements girls wear colorful dresses and the young men try to catch their attention by wearing big cowboy hats and boots. More and more, the Aboriginal way of life is disappearing as he becomes increasingly dependent on the Whitefella who has taken his country into the twentieth century.

Spears are used for hunting. This man trims his spearshaft with a stone scraper hafted on to the handle of a spear-thrower.

A young Aborigine guts a wild-cat. The successful hunter can eat the prized internal organs — the rest is pounded into a mash for the group.

53

Tasmania's extinct Aborigines

There is only one branch of mankind, discernible as a trace, that has become extinct in recent times – the Tasmanian Aborigines. In 1876, Truganini, the last full-blood of her people, died in Oyster Cove, to the south of Hobart. Any account of their life and times is, therefore, history.

When first encountered by Europeans, Tasmanian material culture appeared so rudimentary that they were immediately dubbed the 'representatives of Paleolithic men.' John Lubbock went further and implicitly denied their humanity: 'The Van Diemener and the South American are to the antiquary what the opossum and sloth are to the geologist.'

Both the Tasmanian Aborigines and the Australian Aborigines were paleolithic hunters and gatherers. But the Tasmanians were not as technologically advanced as their brothers on the mainland. They never mastered the technique of shaping and polishing stones to make tools and weapons – a neolithic technique well advanced on the mainland. The Tasmanians never got further than chipping and flaking their stone implements.

The Tasmanian Aborigine could not draw; had no mythology to speak of; their canoes were mere bundles of bark tied together with vegetable fiber; they obtained fire by rubbing one stick in the groove of another, rather than by the relatively more advanced drill method.

Tasmanian origins are obscure – and will probably remain so. It is probable that in ancient times there were at least two periods of migration to the Australian continent from South East Asia; first, a negroid race (distinguished by their dark skin and woolly hair) – the original Tasmanians – who were pushed south in the second wave of migration by the ancestors of the present-day Australian Aborigines who were of different racial stock (their skin is not so dark and their hair straight). Until 11,000 years ago Tasmania was joined to the mainland. But with its separation the Aborigines in that region were isolated from any further racial or cultural contact. And so they remained – a Stone Age people of a most primitive kind – until exploration and settlement of the island in the 18th and 19th centuries.

Tasmania was discovered in 1642 by Abel Tasman who named it Van Diemen's Land, and it does not appear to have been visited by any other European until 1772, when a French expedition explored the coast. It was subsequently visited by the British; and Bass and Flinders first circumnavigated the island in 1798. But there were the voyages of La Perouse (1788) and Bruni d'Entrecasteaux (1791) and then a scientific expedition under Baudin visited the island in 1802. In order to forestall a possible French settlement the British set up an administration in 1804 at Hobart.

We depend for first hand information about the Tasmanians on numerous casual accounts by unskilled observers and a few careful observations made by the one or two Europeans who took the trouble to understand

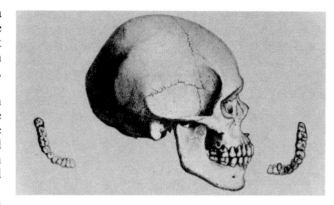

This typical Tasmanian skull belonged to a head preserved in spirit which was brought back to Paris in the late 19th century in order that the brain matter could be studied. When dissected the brain was an amorphous mass. The skull shows marked brow ridge and prognathism. Dental characteristics—notably the commonness of the fifth denticle—are unique to homo sapiens. Nearest surviving relatives are not Australian aborigines but are probably New Caledonians.

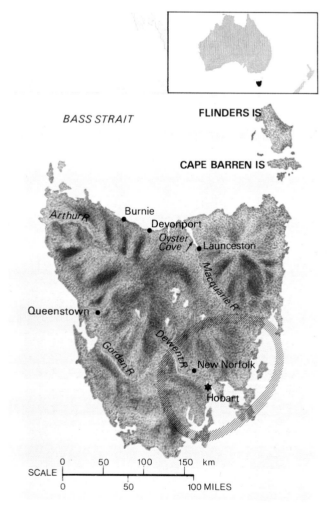

BASS STRAIT

FLINDERS IS

CAPE BARREN IS

Arthur R

Burnie

Devonport

Oyster Cove

Launceston

Macquarie R.

Queenstown

Gordon R.

Derwent R.

New Norfolk

Hobart

SCALE

0   50   100   150   km

0   50   100 MILES

Bessy Clark (below left) and Wapperty, photographed in the 1860's, were two of the last members of the now extinct Tasmanian race.

William Lanney was one of the last Tasmanian Aboriginal males to survive the impact of the white invader. The last male died in 1865.

Truganini, a woman, died in 1876, the last pure blooded member of her ill-fated race — the only race in modern times to disappear completely.

This Queensland Aborigine displays features similar to Tasmanians, suggesting former occupation of mainland Australia by Tasmanian types.

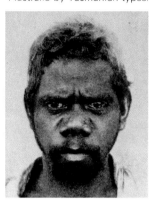

55

By 1847 only forty-seven Tasmanians survived. This photograph shows nine of them on their reserve at Oyster Cove, near Hobart.

Tasmania's extinct Aborigines

A group of Tasmanian
Aborigines was sketched in
front of their temporary
shelters, made of bark,
which served as windbreaks.

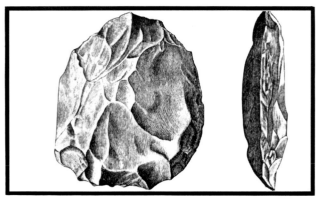

The Tasmanians burned their
dead, then buried them under
grass mounds around which
they constructed a pyramid
of bark strips.

Petit Nicolas who
accompanied Baudin's
expedition to the island in
1802 sketched this
Tasmanian Aborigine woman.

Tasmanian stone culture was
unsophisticated, as this
typical instrument (above),
used for shaping spears and
skinning game, indicates.

(Center right) Tasmanian
canoes were made of bundles
of bark bound together with
coarse grass fiber. They held
about two or three people.

them. From all accounts, the Tasmanian Aborigines were dirty, ugly, short and stocky (about 5 feet 4 inches on average) with black woolly hair often rubbed with ocher. They were completely naked except for the occasional kangaroo skin slung over their shoulders, and the chest, arms and thighs of both male and female were lined with symmetrical scars. They cultivated no crops and lived a nomadic existence. They had no domestic animals, but later, dogs brought by settlers were rapidly assimilated into their economy. The Aborigines grew so close to their dogs that often they were suckled by Aborigine mothers.

Their food depended largely on their location – on the coast they ate shellfish (mussels and oysters); in the interior they hunted kangaroos, wallabies and opossums. To supplement this diet, they ate smaller animals, birds and their eggs, grubs, plants and certain indigenous root vegetables. But the most astonishing fact about their diet is that not since prehistoric times have the Tasmanians eaten fish. This is supported by archaeological evidence and by European observers. The Tasmanians had no fish hooks and no knowledge whatsoever of how to fish.

Their weapons and tools were limited to the spear, the waddy and stones. Their spears, often over 10 feet long, were smoothed and sharpened to a point and the end hardened in fire. All witnesses agree that their agility in handling this weapon was exceptional. It was often held by the toe and dragged along behind, to give the impression of being unarmed, and would suddenly be flicked into the hand. Their other weapon, the waddy, was a short piece of wood about 2 feet long and about an inch wide at the hand held end, thickening out to about 3 inches. This end was slightly rounded and often knobbed. One observer has said, 'It was held by the thinner end and used either as a club or missile. Used for the latter purpose, it was hurled with awful force and certain aim.'

Their inter-tribal wars were frequent, probably over hunting grounds, and became more frequent with the arrival of the British, whose settlements forced many Tasmanian Aborigines off their land. Within the tribe there was no elected or hereditary chief and such leadership as there was was based on courage and prowess in tribal wars.

The Tasmanian's stone tools apparently consisted of stones and pebbles chipped or flaked on one side so as to produce a cutting edge. The stones were used for cutting and sharpening spears and waddies, and for cutting notches on trees to aid climbing. With the stones they also skinned kangaroos and cut their hair. They constructed no houses, only windbreaks rudely formed of tree branches behind which fires were built; one witness says that it was only in the coldest weather that they thought of erecting any kind of shelter at all.

No marriage ceremony was ever described or witnessed by Europeans and polygamy was widely practised, although monogamy existed as well. In either case the Tasmanian women were sorely treated. 'Hard labour is the matrimonial inheritance of the poor gin,' wrote one commentator. 'In travelling, the task of carrying her infant, the food, and all the worldly goods and chattels of the family, devolved upon the wretched woman; whilst her lord with head erect, unburdened except with the shield, the spear and the waddy, walked proudly in advance of his frail tottering slave.' Small wonder that many attached themselves to white protectors. Scarification probably took place at ceremonies initiating puberty.

Opinions as to their intelligence differ, but the view of the Rev. John West, the best of the contemporary commentators, has a ring of common sense: 'their intellectual character is low, yet not so inferior as often described. They appeared stupid when addressed on subjects which had no relation to their way of life; but they were quick and cunning within their own sphere . . .'

In the early years of the colony, despite mutual mistrust Aborigines and colonists were on relatively good terms but as colonists encroached more and more on to Aborigines' territory, relations deteriorated. By 1825 the Aborigines had retreated and never approached the settlers except to attack. To resolve this problem the Governor, Colonel George Arthur, launched his spectacular and expensive Black War – a plan to capture all the Aborigines by herding them into the eastern corner and trapping them in the Tasman Peninsula. The exercise was a complete failure as might be expected from the rugged nature of the country and the Aborigines' familiarity with it. Only one woman with a sleeping child was captured. Colonel Arthur's Black War cost the British Government some £36,000.

What 5,000 armed men failed to do was accomplished by one man, unarmed and almost single handed. Between 1831 and 1836 George Robinson, a missionary who had won the confidence of the Aborigines, succeeded in bringing in, by persuasion alone, all the surviving Aborigines of the island. They were induced to give up their nomadic life, and were settled by the Government on Flinders Island, to the north-east of the mainland. The gesture was well-meant but disastrous.

They were housed and compelled to wear clothes. Their food was provided and they were taught the Christian religion (two services on Sunday and others during the week). Schools were set up to teach arithmetic, geography and history. Deprived of their traditional pursuits, they slowly pined away. In 1847, the remaining 47, from an estimated population of 2,000, were transferred to the mainland. There they rapidly deteriorated through contact with white civilization and alcohol and, in 1865, the last full-blood male Aborigine died. Truganini, the last woman, lingered on alone until 1876. Their fate is to be compared to that of the Patagonians.

Tiwi
Melville and Bathurst Islands

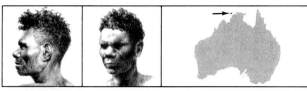

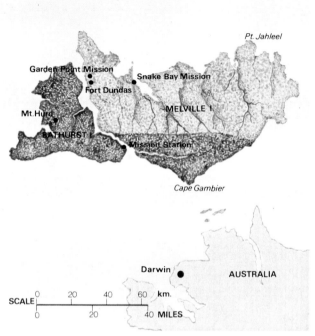

Pt. Jahleel

Garden Point Mission

Snake Bay Mission

Fort Dundas

MELVILLE I.

Mt. Hurd

BATHURST I.

Mission Station

Cape Gambier

Darwin

AUSTRALIA

SCALE

0   20   40   60   km.

0   20   40 MILES

The twin islands of Melville and Bathurst belong to the Northern Territory of Australia and lie some 30 miles off its coast, not far from Darwin, separated from each other only by a narrow channel. From the mainland on a clear day you can see their dim outline – a sub-tropical land of 2,900 square miles of low hill, plain and forest, where natural foodstuffs are to be found in abundance, both on the land and in the surrounding waters. The close-knit Tiwi tribe of just under a thousand members has been lucky to live on islands where nature is generous and the struggle for survival therefore relatively easy.

Until the beginning of this century the Tiwi had the islands almost entirely to themselves. Today they share it with a small number of white missionaries and government representatives. Until this recent contact the Tiwi were also isolated from the rest of Aboriginal Australia, rarely coming into contact with other tribes. Thus the Tiwi, while sharing many aspects of their culture with other Aboriginal peoples, also have developed some which are unique to the islands.

Although many changes have recently occurred due to Western influences, the Tiwi marriage system has always been of traditional central importance. Every Tiwi female

58

The 1,000-strong Tiwi tribe is concentrated around the Mission Station on Bathurst Island and the two Missions on Melville Island.

59

Contact between the two
centers of Tiwi life — on
Bathurst and Melville islands —
is maintained by sturdy
dugouts.

must at all times be married, from birth – indeed, from before her birth – to her death. When a woman reaches puberty, her as-yet-unconceived female children are 'promised' to a man – who thereby becomes a son-in-law to his 'promised-wives' mother. This man will already be an adult when his wives are born, perhaps 25 to 30 years older than them. It follows that a wife is often widowed quite young, whereupon she is at once married – sometimes to a man her own age or even quite a bit younger than herself.

As the Tiwi believe that pregnancy is not only caused by intercourse but also by a 'spirit child' being found by a father and sent by him to its mother (his wife), it follows that a woman must always have a husband, for a child cannot be born unless it is found by its mother's husband. Young Tiwi wives were frequently finding spirit children entering into them, 'made' by younger lovers, but 'sent' to them by their aged husbands – the true 'fathers' of the spirit children.

Wives were, in the past, the major food gatherers and hunters of small game – they were also a mark of a man's prestige. A complex system of intrigue and barter grew up round the practice of 'promising' or 'bestowing' wives-to-be-born (really making an alliance between a son-in-law and a mother-in-law) or in the remarriage of widows. The choice of a son-in-law for one's daughter, or for one's self, is a highly political matter. The bestower usually selects some promising young man around 30, who might make a useful and powerful ally in years to be. The offer of a daughter (as a wife, or as a mother-in-law) usually cements this alliance.

As in financial power-games of the Western world, success breeds success; and whereas a young man might find it very hard to gain his first wife, once he has proved himself by securing two or three wives he might find that others flow in easily. Thus while some men might have had 10 to 20 wives in the past, a few might have remained with none. This does not mean that women greatly outnumber the men, for a woman might well be married several times during her life-time, balancing the fact that a man, though he might have several wives at once, marries much later in life. This marriage system gives the women great security. They are not mere pawns: though a girl's first husband is selected for her, when the time comes for remarriage a widow of character often has influence over her relatives' choice of a new husband.

Today this traditional marriage system is changing under Christian impact. Few men have more than a single wife sharing their house with them and there are many alternative ways of achieving prestige. Marriages of consent between partners much the same age, whether Catholic or pagan, are becoming commoner, but are by no means the rule: a girl may often 'consent' to a marriage that in fact has been arranged for her by relatives in the old manner; or with the additional consent of her arranged-for-husband, she will marry one of her choice.

60

Carved and painted graveposts are prepared for a funeral ceremony. One of the dancers mounts a gravepost in a position suggesting crucifixion.

Preparing for a funeral ceremony — an important Tiwi occasion — an elder touches up his face with white clay with the help of a mirror from a very distant culture.

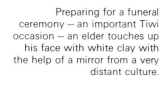

Tiwi boys play with a crocodile's head — its teeth will be sold for the far-off souvenir market. The shed behind is an innovation.

(Above center) A Tiwi youth delves in the sand for turtles eggs. The Tiwi hunt, and collect wild fruits and roots.

Because of recently introduced commercial forestry project and schooling opportunities for all Tiwi children, the Tiwi have given up the nomadic hunting and food gathering life and have settled into three localities – one around the Catholic mission on Bathurst, and the other two at Government establishments on Melville Island. Here the Tiwi have built themselves permanent houses and here they obtain their food of the canned and packaged varieties available to them. Occasionally they may roam the bush for fresh food and for a while return to their traditional life where both men and women hunt for wallabies, lizards and other small land marsupials, crabs, turtle eggs, and oysters; where men fish for a variety of succulent fish and crocodiles or kill wildfowl; and where the women collect yams and wild fruits.

The tribe used to live naked save for penis sheaths for the men and rough bark aprons for the women. Today most men wear loincloths or trousers and women wear skirts made of bought material. Many young Tiwi men now go to work in Darwin, while the older men sell some of the wooden objects they manufacture. This earns the tribe money so that they can buy certain goods – iron axes and knives, food and tobacco, clothing and sometimes mirrors or plates. Tiwi wood-carvings, of high quality, are in several leading Australian museums.

Although many changes have occurred in recent times, the Tiwi still find time to carry out their traditional religious ceremonies: one concerned with the death of a fellow Tiwi, the other with the seasonal changes with the ending of the rains and the beginning of the time of plenty. This was traditionally the time when young men and girls were initiated into adulthood by teaching them the elaborate *kulama yam* rituals. This latter ceremony is not being carried out frequently today, but the funeral ceremony still involves many in its lengthy sequence of activities.

The funeral (*the pukimani*) will take place weeks or months after the burial. During this period the close relatives are in a state of taboo and must remain inactive, save for the making of elaborate carved ceremonial spears, and painted bark baskets. Others meanwhile prepare the funeral posts and the grave area for the final two day ritual. The graveposts are elaborately carved and brightly painted and may be as much as 15 to 20 feet tall. A more important Tiwi will have at least five and some as many as 20. When the posts are completed the two-day ceremonies begin.

Mourners paint their bodies with elaborately colored patterns; they dance ritual and highly creative dances around the grave and the posts, and sing both traditional and new mourning songs. Finally the ghost of the dead Tiwi is satisfied and the *pukimani* ends, the mourners say goodbye to the ghost and ask it not to interfere with the life of the living. A life which used to be troubled by few changes, is today decade by decade disturbed by dramatic and sometimes even traumatic changes.

61

The Peoples of New Guinea

New Guinea is the second largest island in the world – only Greenland is larger. Its length is roughly the distance from London to Moscow or from San Francisco to St Louis. A range of mountains runs the length of the island with peaks exceeding 15,000 feet; within these mountains are many broad, high valleys whose floors vary from 5,000 to 10,000 feet above sea level. The terrain is everywhere very difficult; as well as the central highlands, there are many other mountain ranges which break up much of the inland territory, while the great river systems that drain the mountains form immense swamps and flood plains.

The size and terrain of the island, added to the very simple technology of its inhabitants, go far to explain why it contains such a large number of different cultures and languages. A recent estimate suggests that although the population is only about 3,000,000 there are at least a thousand different languages and dialects in the island. The terrain also explains why so many of these neolithic cultures have survived long into the twentieth century. The western end of New Guinea has, on the coast, long had contact with some of the Indonesian sultanates, and so was nominally incorporated into the Dutch East Indian empire: in the later years of the nineteenth century the Australian colonies, perturbed by the danger of unfriendly neighbors, urged the British government to annex some or all of the eastern half.

It was only the arrival in the north-east of the Germans first as traders and later as rulers that eventually persuaded the British government to act and proclaim a protectorate over the south-east part of the island in 1884. The Dutch, German and British governments then, by negotiation in Europe, defined the boundaries of their respective territories – neat straight lines on the map passing through an island whose interior was completely unknown. The British later handed over their territory, Papua, to the newly founded Commonwealth of Australia and in 1914 the Australians took over German New Guinea after only token opposition.

The origins of the New Guinea population have long been the subject of dispute. Obviously there has been a considerable mixture some time in the past. Skin color, for example, varies from an absolutely matt black that seems to absorb all the available light, found on Buka, to a very delicate light *café au lait* in the Port Moresby area. Usually considerable variation is to be found within a village, as well as between areas. New Guineans differ racially from the Australian Aborigines although it would seem likely that they must in part share the same ancestry. The Negritos, certainly very early inhabitants of South-East Asia, whose remnant is found on isolated islands and in the center of jungles, are another likely component. Certainly there must have been some mixture of later South-East Asian stocks and most recently of Melanesians, probably from the New Hebrides.

In terms of currently accepted theories about language-differentiation, the diversity found in central New Guinea suggests long occupation and comparative isolation. Archaeological work in the island has only started in the last few years, but has already demonstrated that there were people living in the valleys of the central highlands before 10,000 BC. The coastal areas and the off-shore islands seem to have been settled comparatively recently by Melanesian-speaking populations.

Despite the great diversity in race and language, the various societies of New Guinea show certain common characteristics. Apart from some islands such as the Trobriands, New Guinea societies are all without any form of chieftainship or inherited rank and a very aggressive individualism maintains the ideal of equality. There is constant competition for prestige among adult men and each is judged according to his achievements. The political units are small, usually a single village, or in parts of the highlands, a dispersed set of hamlets.

Fighting alternates with periods of truce, and enemies are as important in the social universe as allies; extensive marriages with enemy villages are widespread and the participation of enemies is often vital in ceremonial and exchange. The effective leaders of these minute republics are normally called Big Men, whose skills and prestige make their opinions influential in the community as a whole. Part at least of the prestige of a Big Man comes from his relationship with other groups, both ally and enemy. In such external relations Big Men count on the total support of their own group which they represent. Throughout the island, rivalry and aggression are expressed not only in fighting between groups, but also in exchanges of pigs, wealth and crops both between and within groups.

The great ceremonial exchanges with neighboring groups had and still have few economic functions, to our way of thinking, but serve as huge displays of wealth in pigs and shell valuables. These are given, with much bombastic speech-making, to neighbors – and in due course the neighbors have to make a similar return. The principle in operation in such exchanges is that of equality, and an individual or group incapable of giving as well as it receives appears worthless and shamed in the eyes of all those participating. The production of pigs and food and the acquisition of valuables is thus given an enormous stimulus. But it is worth noting that though, as is true in our society, it is important for the individual to produce and accumulate goods and wealth, to get prestige, in New Guinea, a man must give these things away – whereas we get prestige by *keeping* and displaying our acquisitions.

The traditional religions of New Guinea are very diverse. A whole array of spirits and ancestors are believed to influence the fortunes of man on the earth and are considered generally necessary for success and for plentiful crops. Human skills are highly valued but success demands help from the spirits as well. The after

Sorong

Fakfak

INDON

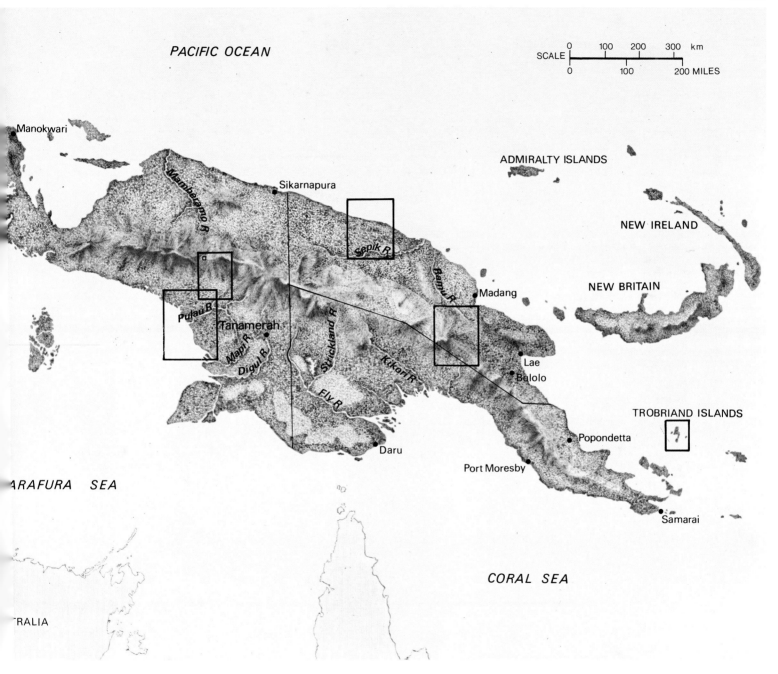

PACIFIC OCEAN

SCALE
0   100   200   300   km
0   100   200 MILES

Manokwari

ADMIRALTY ISLANDS

Mamberamo R.

Sikarnapura

NEW IRELAND

Sepik R.

Ramu R.

Madang

NEW BRITAIN

Pulau R.

Tanamerah

Mapi R.

Digul R.

Strickland R.

Kikori R.

Lae
Bulolo

Fly R.

TROBRIAND ISLANDS

Popondetta

Daru

ARAFURA   SEA

Port Moresby

Samarai

CORAL SEA

'RALIA

life is usually considered to be much like the present and the idea of punishment for sins in the world was everywhere absent, before the introduction of Christianity. Religion is in fact concerned with moderate material prosperity, and little else: especially in the lowland and coastal areas it provides the occasion for most spectacular ceremonies.

These are occasions of great enjoyment and devoid of any religious hush, although offerings to ancestors and spirits usually play an important part. Carvings, paint-

ings, masks and huge ceremonial houses, all of the highest artistic quality are typical of these cults. The advent of the Europeans – with political domination, the introduction of cash and the work of Christian missions – has weakened or destroyed much of the traditional culture. The desperate desire to come to terms with the radically changed situation is epitomized by the cargo cults: in New Guinea, as in Melanesia, many still believe that conversion to Christianity will bring great wealth in cargo ships. They are bitterly disappointed.

63

Asmat
New Guinea

An Asmat wears a bone nose-
ornament and face paint —
these will frighten his
enemies and add to his
courage.

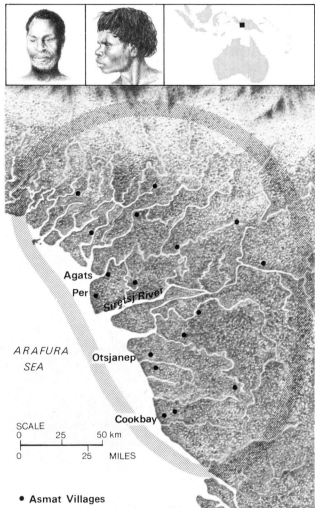

ARAFURA
SEA

Agats
Per
Siretsj River

Otsjanep

Cookbay

SCALE
0   25   50 km

0   25   MILES

● Asmat Villages

On the south-west coast of New Guinea a vast tropical rain-forest, cut by a thousand rivers, reaches to the very edge of the sea. It is flat land where, in a greenish light, creeks lose their way among the trees, while close to the ocean, the ceaseless rhythm of ebb and flood blurs the borderline between water and land. Swamp forest becomes tidal forest and at high tide the trees stand in brackish water, only later revealing the mud on which they stand. Here the Asmat live in an isolation that is infrequently interrupted by visitors – almost inaccessible from the sea and protected at the rear by the range of snow-topped mountains. The Asmat culture sharply reflects both this isolation and the oppressive, uncompromising nature of their environment.

There are no stones in the alluvial mud of the forests and the few stone axes that the Asmat possess are obtained from the highland tribes by barter over a long route. Pottery is unknown and all food is roasted over an open fire. The basis of all Asmat culture and industry is the wood that is all around them. The *sago* tree is not 65

To become a new member of the community a woman must be reborn. Here she is carried as though an infant.

A ritual bonding of clan-friendship is enacted on the ceremonial ground in front of the long-house.

merely the main source of food, but also the most basic raw-material. Houses, hunting weapons (the Asmat hunt wild pigs), canoes and paddles (they fish and catch shrimps in the rivers) and of course their fires – all are utterly dependent on wood.

To the Asmat, tree and man are symbolically identical; man's feet are the roots of a tree, and the trunk of a tree is the man's body. The fruit of a tree is used as a metaphor for a man's head. And this, in particular, has profound implications for Asmat culture. The Asmat are head-hunters; any fruit-eating animal symbolizes this concept and birds, such as the black king cockatoo and the hornbill, and the flying fox are all therefore honored in paintings and decorations.

The praying mantis similarly has great symbolic meaning. The female insect often bites off the head of the male directly after, or during, mating. It seems to the Asmat a natural justification for the head-hunting culture. Among the Asmat it is the women who actively encourage and incite the men to hunt heads, shaming their husbands in public should the family collection of skulls be too small. The heads are of members of other Asmat groups.

A central feature of Asmat culture is the *yeu* ceremonial house which is the center of all festival and dance activities of the village. Often it is called the bachelor house because unmarried men and boys spend the greater part of the day within its walls. Villages are normally divided into quarters, each of which has its own ceremonial house. These houses are large, about 100 feet long and 20 feet wide, and every four or five years they must be rebuilt since wooden structures quickly deteriorate in the rainy, tropical climate. And when the new house is ready the ritual of inauguration begins.

All the men except the *yeu* leaders (the senior members of the house) and a number of drummers leave the house and take part in the dancing that goes on outside. Inside,

(Opposite) Asmat men from a neighboring clan mimic the sleep of an infant. This ritual follows the ceremony that binds the clans in friendship.

a huge cylinder of palm leaves, sometimes 10 feet high, is placed in the middle opposite the central hearth. This container is then filled with larvae of the capricorn beetle by each male member of the community. This represents the 'sago tree of life'. The women then enter the house and dance around this symbol, followed by the men. A guest of honor, or a prominent *yeu* member then slits open the palm leaf container and the larvae flow out in a long stream. Their abundance symbolizes new life emerging from the 'tree of life' to vitalize the community.

On the occasion when a ritual adoption of men from another village takes place, the women again play an important part. The women line up one behind the other, and the men who are to be adopted crawl through the tunnel formed by the women's legs. In this way the men act out their rebirth as new members of the community. It corresponds to the ceremony that consecrates the new *yeu* house, since there the 'sago tree of life' is symbolized as the source of life; similarly, the women in the adoption ritual represent the source of new members of the community.

According to one of the Asmat creation myths, Fumeripits, a traditional hero, created the first *yeu* house by drawing an outline of it near the coast. He had soon built it, but it was empty. Fumeripits then began to carve statues of people from the trees, until the whole house was full of carved figures. Then he carved a drum from another piece of wood and as he started to play, the figures came to life and danced in the Asmat way. Their feet were slightly apart, their knees wavered to the rhythm of the drum and slowly the dancers advanced with small steps. Thus Fumeripits was not only the creator of life, but also the first carver and the first drummer.

It is said too that Fumeripits was the Great Head-hunter. After one long, fierce battle he killed a huge crocodile that had tried to destroy the newly created *yeu* house. The crocodile was cut in pieces and cast in many 67

An Asmat enters the all-male long-house which, like the other houses, is built on stilts close to the river.

Rivers are both highways and fishing-grounds in the Asmat forests. Here villagers net and spear cat fish.

directions. From each of these pieces sprang the many kinds of men: the black, the brown and the white. And this myth expresses another fundamental characteristic of Asmat culture; in the creation of life something must be destroyed. Death is a prerequisite of life. It is a corroboration of the fertility element of head-hunting and its natural consequences, cannibalism, which itself is a means to ensure that the vital essence of the victim is reabsorbed.

The most striking examples of Asmat art are carvings of *bis* – ancestor poles from the mangrove trees. The death of any important person, or someone who has wealthy relatives, is marked by carving such a figure and a public ceremony in which obligations are undertaken to avenge the death of the relative represented by the *bis*. The Asmat believe that no one ever dies a natural death; they are either killed in actual fighting or by magical means. The mangrove trunk is carved to symbolize two or more

68

Children of Asmat head-hunters often go to school in one of the Indonesian administered villages near the coast.

Asmat men rest their heads on
the skulls of enemies believing
that this will appease
ancestral spirits.

ancestor figures. After being displayed for some time, the *bis* are taken to the forest where they are left to decay. In this way the supernatural powers will promote the growth of sago trees.

Whenever a woodcarver carves a human figure out of wood, he repeats the mythological creation performed by Fumeripits. Yet he knows that however good his carving may be, or however long he may drum, he will never transmute his carving into a living being. The same applies to all Asmat who attend the sacred rituals and dances with greater fervor. The tree and the man are conceptual facsimiles; the Asmat are men of the world. Even the greatest and most venerated woodcarver has to do his own sago pounding, his own fishing and hunting.

In every village, whether large or small, the woodcarver is known to everyone. He is distinguishable from other men in that his skills enable him to do more than just build houses, canoes and weapons. The rest of the community will go to the carver for anything special, such as a shield decorated with designs representing ancestors, canoe paddles with decorated blades and of course, the *bis*. A commission to do such work will be informal; the carver will take as long as he sees fit. Payment is normally made in the form of food, tools or tobacco; but the real reward will be derived from prestige.

Until recent years stone axes, animals' teeth and boars' tusks were the only Asmat tools. Oyster shells were used to scrape and smooth surfaces. But now, as more sophisticated implements filter through from the highlands, the Asmat are also found to use iron axes, chisels made from flattened nails and steel knives. The *bis*, which traditionally were only taken into the forest, have on occasions been sold to white men; and these bring in rewards that are far more tangible and immediate than those of former days when the supernatural powers of *bis* ancestors caused the sago trees to grow better.

69

Abelam
New Guinea

An Abelam villager carries an
enormous feather head-dress.
It represents his *nggwalndu* —
the major spirit of his clan.

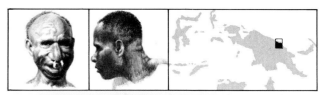

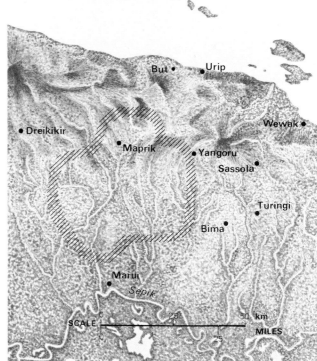

BISMARCK SEA

But •   • Urip

• Dreikikir

Wewak •

• Maprik   Yangoru •
                     Sassola •

                              Turingi •

                    Bima •

Marui •
    Sepik

SCALE   25°   50 km

                          MILES

The proud and aggressive tribes of the Sepik River
area were largely unknown to Europeans until the
beginning of this century. As explorers began to
penetrate the area, news of these remarkable people and
their marvelous artistic talent spread far and wide.
Contact with Western colonialism, money and trade has
greatly weakened tradition, especially on the coast, but
inland, custom has survived to a much greater extent. One
people amongst whom traditional ways are still strong is
the Abelam who live about 20 miles from the Sepik
River. Compared with life on the river – where food in the
form of fish and natural sago can be had with only the
effort of collection – survival in the Abelam hills requires
much greater efforts. Yams require constant care to
ensure good yields, and domestic pigs, which are the main
source of protein, themselves require feeding. Food
production has therefore developed an elaborate and   71

Abelam New Guinea

efficient procedure and involves complex rituals and social ceremonies.

The Abelam are not racially homogeneous and before colonial control inclined to political independence. Villages tend to be large, numbering 350 to 1,000 inhabitants – and each controls its own ceremonials by decision-making debates open to all and swayed by the most eloquent. Most important communal activity is organized by these influential men of high prestige, called Big Men, the maintenance of whose status requires constant efforts.

Male Sepik society appears to be based on a continual struggle between highly individualistic men for prestige and for the influence over other men that this prestige confers. Men behave in a proud and aggressive manner. They are quick to find in another's behavior an affront to their dignity. Noisy quarrels are frequent, and in the days of inter-village fighting often led to real violence and killing. The set battles between villages seem to have been more sporting occasions with only a few casualties. Within the village, despite the extremely violent manner in which men habitually behave, actual woundings are rare and compensation must be paid for any damage done. But both extravagant behavior and social restraint are demanded, so that rivalry and competition within the village, even if controlled, are amply expressed in symbolic fighting and more often through the competitive giving of gifts.

The yam cult of the Abelam is a fine example of male competition expressed in symbolic form. Yams are the preferred food of the Abelam, who recognize at least a hundred different varieties, and they have been skilful in selecting and developing varieties suitable for different terrains. The south-western Abelam, who live at the high density of 200 people per square mile, cultivate the broad river flats, which, although fertile, are liable to flooding and have a high water table – conditions usually fatal to yam cultivation. The Abelam have, however, developed

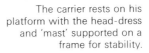

With the head-dress in place, the carrier lies on a platform while his face is painted to identify with *nggwalndu*.

The carrier rests on his platform with the head-dress and 'mast' supported on a frame for stability.

a water-tolerant yam, *asagwa*, which produces very large tubers and forms a dominant part of their supply.

In the northern part of the area, where the terrain is more hilly, the Abelam cultivate long thin tubers, which form the focus of the male cult of fertility and competition. These *wapi* tubers have been recorded with lengths of nearly 12 feet, although 9 feet is a more usual size for the best specimens, while 6-foot-long tubers are plentiful in most years. The growing of these long yams is surrounded by taboo and ritual and they are the focus of a phallic cult. Each adult man has to purify himself from past sexual contact and maintain a complete taboo on sex and eating meat for about six months from the first operations of planting until the tubers are harvested. Yams are grown in special gardens into which only men observing the taboos may go, and which are subject to a series of magical procedures designed to improve the yams. The rituals are carried out in a small hut actually in the garden; ancestors' skulls, long stones and carvings, representing the ancestors, nature and the clan spirits respectively, form a shrine to the magic.

The aim is always to produce the longest yams. When the harvest comes each man decorates his finest tubers, giving them masks and other decorations which associate them with the spirits. They are then displayed in a great harvest festival, designed to increase the prestige of both the village and the individual grower. No man may eat or use his own sacred yams, which must all be given away. Each man has an exchange partner, and both will record the lengths of yams exchanged by cutting tallies so that the record of several years' exchanges is preserved. The idea is always to give longer yams than you receive, thus demonstrating your superiority to your partner.

Competition is intense and a man who fails to maintain his own in these exchanges for a period of years loses prestige within his village or outside. Apart from this regular exchange, the presentation of yams is also used as an aggressive act: a man may present another whom he

A carved plank carved in relief with human heads is erected at the base of the facade of a ceremonial house.

(Below center) Flooding of the Sepik River makes the people build their ceremonial houses on stilts.

Initiators painting panels to line an initiation chamber. They are under strict taboo and work in a fenced-off area just beneath the ceremonial house.

suspects of adultery with his wife with a huge yam indicating in his speech that the other being so interested in sex will be unable to grow a yam of decent size and therefore be shamed. So, in providing a stimulus to male competition the yam cult has done much to refine methods of cultivation and ensure their transmission from generation to generation.

In the yam cult women are excluded from the gardens and any contact with female sexuality is believed to be disastrous for the yams. This very strict sexual separation is typical of many simple societies but is particularly prominent in New Guinea and in the Sepik. It is not so much a matter of men excluding women but rather that the differences between the sexes are elaborated enormously, particularly in ceremonial matters. It is almost true to say that there are two cultures, one for the men and one for the women; each has its own rituals from which the other is excluded. The men tend to make more of a splash and at first sight the women appear very modest and even down-trodden in their manner. But greater familiarity with village life shows how the sexes are complementary and completely interdependent. The men themselves believe that women, by their very nature, are endowed with powers of creativity and mystical influence that the men can only acquire through the performance of elaborate ritual and the observance of onerous taboos.

One of the most important of the exclusively female rituals is that of first menstruation, where girls have their bellies, breasts and upper arms cicatrized. While the girl is held by her mother's brother (who among the Abelam is regarded as a mother), the designs are cut into her skin by women. Thereafter the women take over the men's ceremonial ground and for the rest of the day perform rituals about which the men endlessly speculate but from which they are absolutely excluded; all they can hear is the noise of excitement and merriment. The next day the girl, with her head shaved and profusely decorated, enters into a period of some months in which her new womanhood is celebrated. She does no work but visits every household in the village and in neighboring villages and is everywhere flattered and entertained with the finest food. This period ends with marriage, housekeeping and childbirth and admission into the full status of an adult woman.

The Sepik peoples have since their discovery been justly renowned for their art of which there is a great deal in European and American museums, mostly originally produced for use in the cult of male initiation. In the Sepik region this usually involves the passage of young men through a whole series of ceremonies. Each of these uses many carved and painted objects to symbolize complex ideas involving the fundamental values and beliefs of the culture. The relationship between man and man, as well as that between man and the spirits is thus dramatized in a manner which has great impact on the initiate and

(Right) Five *nggwalndu* faces stare from this typical ceremonial house. The faces symbolize clan spirits and at the top is a single face representing a female witch.

Abelam New Guinea

Initiators of Wingei village painting a *nggwalndu* figure for the final ceremony of the cycle. Behind are some minor figures awaiting painting.

An Iatmul of the Sepik River holds out a *Mwai* mask. The nose extension ending in a totemic bird is typical of their art.

This shield for the prow of a canoe from the upper Sepik terrifies the enemy and protects the canoe's occupants.

76

Initiators parade as spirits in basketry head-dresses and body paintings which are decorated with bird of paradise plumes.

An ash-covered senior man rushes round the ceremonial ground, taking on all the dangers of the ritual and the spirits.

Aswaga and other yams on display. Those classified as male are painted with a lizard. Yam display is a form of competition among the Abelam.

audience. These ceremonies are held on the dancing ground, the male focus of the village, and usually dominated by the ceremonial house in which the sacred images are stored and in which initiation displays are organised.

Among the Abelam there are eight different ceremonies each of which is said to be showing the initiates the *nggwalndu*. The *nggwalndu*, whose faces appear on the bottom of the facade of the ceremonial house, are spirits associated with each of the patrilineal clans which make up the village. The initiates are shown a display inside the ceremonial house which they are told is the *nggwalndu*, at the next ceremony they are told "we were only fooling last time but this time you are actually going to see the *nggwalndu*" and so on until at the eighth ceremony of the series they are actually shown the huge carved figures that stand for the *nggwalndu*. After the display the initiators, with elaborate body paint and decorations, parade from the ceremonial house as if they were the spirits themselves.

The great ceremonies, with their displays and parades have the air of a great secular festival; and everyone enjoys themselves, except possibly the initiates who may get a mild beating as the price of seeing the display. Indeed, actual religious acts are not very obvious; a few invocations may be sung and some of the very plentiful food may be flung down by the ancestors' stones, but on the whole enjoyment seems to predominate and many love affairs blossom during the all-night dancing. Yet this impression is misleading; sometimes for months before the actual ceremonial the initiators having been preparing the display and every stage of the operation is controlled by ritual. The process of preparing the display is in fact a slow accumulation of supernatural power which is released at the actual ceremonial.

The last stage is the most sacred, that of the actual painting of any carvings to be shown and of flat panels used to line the initiation chamber, and for other decoration. The painting phase is started by all the initiators purifying themselves from past sexual contact. They have to observe a total taboo on sex until all the

Abelam man wears a basketry mask — semi-sacred representation of the spirit. When dressed in these masks, they can engage in horseplay.

Abelam New Guinea

An adolescent Abelam girl
smiles modestly over the scars
of her initiation into womanhood. Her string 'skirt' is the
traditional form of dress.

Skulls of ancestors, phallic stones and — on the right — carved symbols of clan spirits in the shape of a yam, lie in a big shrine.

painting is finished. The designs are all those used by the ancestors, and the artists, by using the ordinary earth paints to recreate ancestral designs, are recreating the supernatural power of the creators of the ceremonies themselves. By being painted in a correct ancestral design, the secular paint becomes a powerful substance carrying with it the benefit of the ceremony. Such paint is rubbed into the skin of the initiates. It is the final stage of preparation, the painting, that generates the supernatural power that the ceremony itself releases.

But all power has its dangers, and while the initiators and the visitors, who come in hundreds from both enemy and allied villages, are enjoying the festival, the supernatural dangers are taken on by two senior men who live in the ceremonial house until the display is dismantled many months later, after the next long yam display. These men must observe the strictest taboos for the whole of this period, only drinking warm muddy water and eating dry roasted yams. They too appear at the ceremony, but in contrast to the decorations and face-paint worn by everyone else they are naked and covered in ashes; men spit as they pass to free themselves of any danger that even seeing them might have conveyed. They eat alone, cooking for themselves, no one will share their fire or touch them.

The most spectacular of the public manifestations of the *nggwalndu* found among the southern Abelam are the huge feather head-dresses, carried by adult men who do in this context become the *nggwalndu*. These head-dresses are shown in all paintings of the *nggwalndu* as red triangles above the head. The feathers used to make them are the breast feathers of small birds, and tens of thousands of such feathers are needed to make the largest of the head-dresses. To be able to make one a man must mobilize all his friends and relatives, and only the most influential men have large enough networks of such influence to be able to borrow the necessary feathers. The feathers are used to build up a design on a light cane framework and the whole construction is surmounted by a 'mast' of pith some 25 feet high in which further feathers are stuck. Split cane rings are sewn into the men's hair well in advance, and the head-dress is fixed to these with all the weight being taken on the head: carrying the head-dress is a difficult task requiring quick movements forwards and backwards to keep the structure balanced – a bar at the bottom gives the wearer some control, but basically it is the head-dress that is wearing the man rather than the other way around.

One of the most astonishing aspects of the rich ceremonial and art so typical of the Sepik cultures is the sheer amount produced. Most Sepik cultures, despite their traditional stone tools and simple technology, have evolved such efficient systems for exploitation of their environments that they can afford the time and effort for such repeated magnificence. The people believe that the ceremonies are essential if they are to prosper.

79

Abelam initiates seek rebirth by crawling through one of these carvings to emerge from the other streaked with paint.

Jalé
New Guinea Highlands

Men never venture far from
their home village without
their bows and arrows. They
wear several hundred loops of
split liana vine.

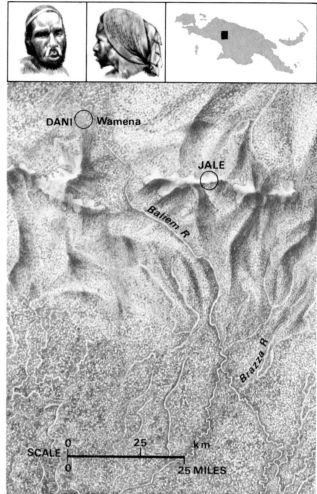

The Jalé people who inhabit the highlands of New Guinea, east of the Baliem Valley, accept war as part of their way of life. It is a bloody business, yet wars are waged mercilessly against neighbors of the same village, against villages of the same valley and even against settlements in other regions. Hostilities may last as long as a generation – though interspersed with periods of truce – or peter out in a single day. Raiding parties loose arrows at a startled foe in the rainforests, or lay siege to an enemy village. Although deaths are limited by the taboos that surround all Jalé conflicts, the dead may still be subjected to further spite – the supreme act of Jalé vengeance is to eat the bodies of slain foe.

Anthropologists have found a generally high level of violence in societies where boys grow up in intimate association with their mothers, in homes where the male elders, especially fathers, do not take part. Other ethnological research suggests that where small kin groups operate as relatively independent political units, warfare within the society is a common means of resolving 81

The Dani and the Jalé both fight frequent wars in the Highlands of New Guinea – but the Jalé alone eat the dead.

Jalé New Guinea Highlands

This battle scene shows a group of Jalé warriors rushing fiercely toward enemy positions in the hills.

Ambushed at a river crossing in the evening this warrior lay in the water until morning when his kinsmen took his body to be cremated.

The medicine man treats a warrior hit by an arrow with curative chants and blowing. Rattan curass and protective nets hang around his neck

conflict. Both findings apply to the Jalé.

First, young boys, separated from the community of the men's house until their initiation, are socialized in a female environment. Secondly, the different wards of a village are not integrated into a central system of headmanship. No political cooperation exists until they are threatened by hostility from other villages. These are the critical factors which, at least partially, determine the bellicosity and violence of the Jalé.

No specific hypothesis can be given to explain the cannibalism. It is certain, however, that no understanding can be achieved by applying precepts of Western thought. In a missionary's travelogue, published 70 years ago, the author recounted: 'Once, when told by a European that the practice of eating human flesh was a most degraded habit, the cannibal answered, "Why degraded? You people eat sheep and cows and fowls, which are all animals of the lowest order; and we eat man, who is great and above all. It is you who are degraded!"'

Among the Jalé, blood feuds may be provoked by a killing in retaliation for a wrong. The wrong could be adultery, theft or failure to pay compensation (in the form of a pig) for a killing. A kin group which can easily rally support may refuse such compensation if it is for the killing of a relative. Negotiated settlements occur most frequently when the aggrieved parties live in the same village and all are threatened by a common, outside enemy.

Wars are not waged for territorial gains or for the suppression of political or religious beliefs. Rather, wars result from a man avenging an injury – to himself or a kinsman – by an assault on one of the 'offender's' clan. The cause of both is taken up by two 'men of the arrow's stem' who rally their respective clans for war and are subsequently held responsible for all deaths suffered by their supporters, both on the battlefield and in clandestine ambushes.

The length of the war will depend upon the outcome of the initial encounter between warring parties and the distance between enemy villages. In any event Jalé warfare is not continuous. During the ceasefires both sides are in a constant state of readiness to counter any surprise attack. After several weeks of fighting the threat of famine will enforce a truce. During this time small bands of kinsmen of a victim whose death went unavenged on the battlefield will venture into enemy territory. A successful raiding party will return with a seized pig. It is revenge action of this kind that often precipitates the resumption of open warfare.

Fighting on the battlefield follows a pattern of haphazardly coordinated engagements, relying on the tactics of 'shoot and run.' This technique is for a warrior to advance as far as the terrain affords him cover, discharge an arrow or two, and then run back to escape enemy retaliation. When one side has been forced to retreat to its village, the fighting turns into sniping from behind

Travel in the rugged terrain of the Jalémo is often an uncertain enterprise. The rivers, swollen by heavy rainfall, frequently sweep away the crude bridges.

huts and fences. Women and children always leave the village if an invasion is imminent, to take refuge with friends and relatives elsewhere.

As a last resort the men retreat into the men's house which is protected by taboo from being burnt. When a battle has reached this stage the victorious side often plunder and burn family huts. A catastrophe of this nature is followed by the defeated side abandoning the village, and the war ceases. But hostilities linger on until a formal peace ceremony reconciles the principal parties. Arranging this ceremony, which involves the ritual slaughter and eating of a pig, may take years of informal negotiations between people who have relatives on both sides. Afterwards, village dances and pig exchanges on a large scale consolidate the end of the war.

Cannibalism is not normally tolerated in wars between neighboring villages of the same valley. 'People whose face is known must not be eaten,' say the Jalé, and the few incidents when this tradition has been violated are remembered as acts of tragic perversion. But in wars between villages which are separated by such boundaries as a mountain ridge, cannibalistic revenge is an integral part of the conflict. Such inter-regional wars last much longer than local conflicts.

During these long periods the tactics of warfare are different. Open confrontation in battle is keenly avoided and revenge parties seek instead to surprise lone hunters or small groups of women working in the fields or gardens. The geography favors similarly long-lasting military alliances, which have a stability quite unlike the shifting allegiances that kinship and trading create in local affairs.

The enigmatic nature of cannibalism has invited many writers to speculate on its origin. Aristotle attributed its occurrence among tribes around the Black Sea to their wild bestiality and morbid lust. Until now it has often been argued that the rejection of cannibalism is the first step into civilization. Even now little is known about the nutritional and social aspects. Few anthropologists have been able to study its practice before missions and colonial governments had eradicated a custom they considered evil. Distorted ideas about this custom are apt, therefore, to reflect, not scientific understanding, but the prejudices of Western culture. Among the Jalé, cannibalism has great symbolic significance in addition to a dietary value. As an act of supreme vengeance it is a consequence of certain conditions which determine the degree of aggression and retaliation tolerated by their culture.

The size of Jalé settlements varies from two dozen huts to more than 100. Each hut has a circular wall of wooden planks, and four central poles support a conical roof made from pandanus leaves or the bark of the casuarina tree—all lashed together with vines. The entrance is a rectangular opening that can be closed with one or two boards. Both the ground-floor, raised one or two feet from the earth, and the sleeping platform, built three to five feet higher, contain a fireplace set between central poles.

All villages except the smallest are made up of two or more neighborhoods or wards, each comprising a large men's house and a cluster of smaller family huts built around it. A family hut is the home of a married woman, her unmarried daughters, and her young sons who have not yet been initiated into the men's house. In a polygynous marriage co-wives may keep a joint household but more often each lives in a hut of her own. The men's house, also called the sacred house, is the domicile of all initiated males. As the center of much ritual activity it is taboo to females and uninitiated boys.

The Jalé make their gardens by a technique known as slash-and-burn agriculture. A piece of land is replanted after a long fallow period during which brushwood has grown where previous cultivation had removed the original forest. Like other New Guinea Highland people the Jalé reserve most of their gardens for the sweet potato – which constitutes about 80 per cent of their vegetable diet. The remainder comes from taro, yam, and a variety of cultivated and wild-growing plants, including several leafy herbs, millet, sugar cane, banana, cucumber, ferns, and pandanus. Other cultivated or semi-cultivated plants provide the men's penis gourd, the women's grass apron, and the yarn used to make nets. Bamboo is used for water containers, pandanus for rain hoods and mats, reeds for arrow shafts, wood for arrow points, digging sticks and adze handles, and vines for all binding purposes and the construction of cuirasses and the men's rattan dress.

The women gather insects, lizards, mice, and frogs, while the men hunt birds, bats and a number of small mammals such as the tree kangaroo, cuscus and giant rats. Depending upon the kind of food to be prepared the Jalé steam their food with hot stones (in an earth oven or in banana leaf wrappings), bake it in hot ashes or roast it in the fire. An elaborate code, enforced by ritual sanctions against any offender, defines the range of foodstuffs that must not be eaten by males or by females respectively. This code may apply throughout life, on specific occasions, or during certain periods, such as after a boy's initiation or a girl's menarche.

In addition to the dog – kept mainly as a pet but sometimes used in hunting – the pig is the only domesticated animal. For the Jalé the pig is much more than a nutritional resource and a trade object. It represents an instrument for the validation of all important social relationships. Every major event in a person's life cycle, the settlement of serious disputes and the ratification of a peace agreement, all require the exchange of pigs.

For the Jalé infant the first year of life is spent in uninterrupted bodily contact with its mother, hanging in a big net on her back during the day and cuddled in her arms when she sleeps. Toward the end of the fourth

A bird's eye view of the village of Pasikni where the anthropologist lived. Note the separate groups of small family huts built around the larger men's houses.

Jalé men are forced to ford a river in full spate as their rickety bridges have been torn apart by the torrents of water.

House building brings together kinsmen and neighbors. When the owner has collected all necessary materials, a small group of men builds a hut in a single day.

85

Women returning from a dance
celebrating a victory in war.
Every dance is an occasion
for making gifts of live pigs
and pork.

year – the time when its mother stops breast-feeding – a child begins to walk about alone. Although boys spend less time with their mothers and sisters after reaching the age of seven or eight, the most dramatic change in their lives occurs between their eleventh and thirteenth years. An elaborate ceremony then separates them from their mother's home and incorporates them into the community of the men's house. From then on they receive their education and training exclusively from their elder co-residents, and by the age of 15 or 16 they have had considerable practice as gardeners, hunters, and craftsmen. For the girls a brief puberty rite marks their first menstruation, which usually occurs when they are between 17 and 19 years old.

Sexual intercourse is forbidden for a girl until she has had her menarche, and a belief that during adolescence intercourse would damage his vitality effectively discourages the Jalé youth from seeking sexual encounters before he has reached adulthood. Since most girls marry before their menarche and intercourse with a married woman entails the risk of severe punishment by the offended husband, a young man has little opportunity for sexual intercourse until he marries. Strict restrictions continue throughout married life. As soon as a woman becomes pregnant, her husband ceases to sleep in his family hut. The taboo extends for about four years after the birth of the child – a method of birth control.

The Jalé believe that every human being possesses a soul or spirit whose growth and decay parallels the changing condition of the body and which departs the body at death. Although the Jalé perform certain rites to ensure its departure, especially at the cremation of the corpse, they fear the ghosts only of those who have died by violence. The medicine men, however, know magic rituals that can relieve the malevolence of such spirits.

The Jalé people divide their population into two marriage classes. Marriage can be undertaken only with someone from the opposite section. This is the sole purpose of the classification. Every person also belongs to a sib, another social category which gives everybody a surname. This name, like the marriage class, follows that of the father. Although people with the same surname may live in many different areas of the Jalé country, they believe in descent from a common ancestor.

Initiation and marriage are complementary processes in the organization of social relationships. When a girl marries she leaves her natal house to take up residence among her husband's kinsmen. Since her children belong to her husband's lineage, her procreative faculty is 'lost' to her own descent group. A boy's initiation into the men's house signifies his membership of his own lineage. Pig exchanges give symbolic expression to these steps. A man presents his wife's kinsmen with the pig that validates his marriage, and the father or elder brothers of an initiate give a pig to his mother's kinsmen, thereby ratifying his incorporation into their descent group.

Old woman who is in
mourning for the death
of her daughter-in-law
comforts her orphaned
grandson.

The Jalé love 'garden parties'
(above centre) where they
consume huge quantities. This
scene follows the building of a
men's house.

Competitive games improve a boy's skill in handling his weapon. The target, a ball cut from a banana tree, represents the enemy.

Asaro Valley People
New Guinea

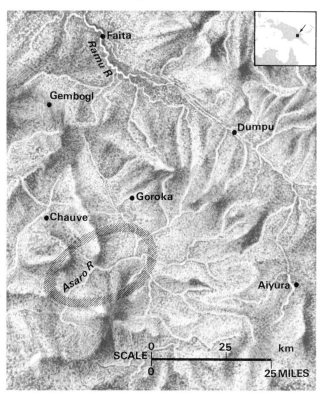

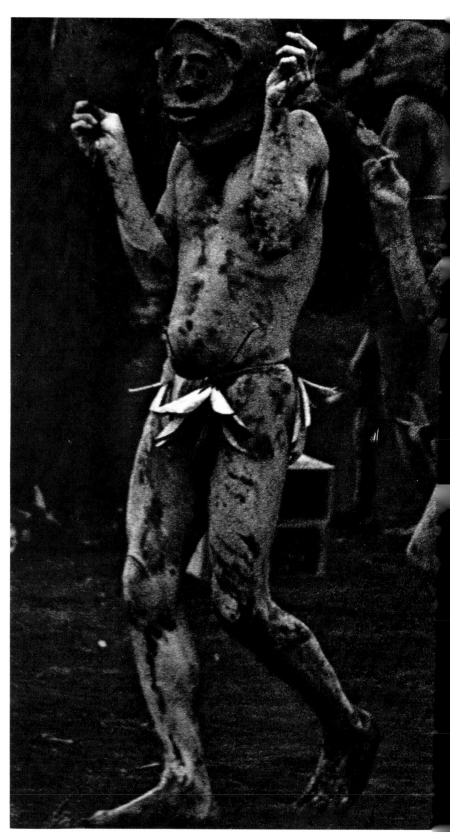

Theatricality infuses man in the Asaro Valley . . . Suddenly, in the afternoon peace of the village, a middle-aged man runs amok. If you were a visitor, among the Gururumba of the upper Asaro Valley in New Guinea, he would probably demand anything of yours that caught his eye: a bowl, a bit of soap, a knife. You should obligingly hand it over. This sudden break-out from normal behavior often occurs in those highland villages. The 'wild pig' makes fierce demands for miscellaneous objects, which are given to him at once.

When he has a good-sized bag of wooden arrowheads, skeins of string, pieces of tobacco and soap and cloth, knives, ropes, plates he vanishes into the forest. After a few days he returns without his bag of treasures: he has destroyed them all, by burning or burying in some secret place, and with the tensions thus worked out of his system, he returns to his normal life. Nobody criticizes or rebukes: his behavior is completely forgotten. But before very long, some other man – it's never a woman – will be going 'wild pig' in his turn.

This behavior-pattern arises from the stress generated by the 'materialism' of Gururumba society. Emotional and social life is almost entirely built round exchange. It is not the things themselves that matter. The strictly economic function of a market is less important than the actual activity of display and exchange, whereby obligations are discharged and relationships established. This creates stress for the man in debt, tormented by his

89

The villagers of Kiminivi, in the
Asaro Valley, sometimes stage
their mud dance for visitors.
The men cake themselves with
mud, and put on masks.

Asaro Valley People New Guinea

Weeks before the festival the men begin building their masks in the valley below the village. Seeds and nuts represent teeth.

On the special day the men smear their bodies with mud and let it cake and dry. They perfect and compare their masks.

inability to control the patterns of exchange, so he breaks out, revenging himself by accumulating such objects and then destroying them. He has asserted himself: he is a man again.

The Gururumba have neighbors who show a similar theatricality. The village of Kiminivi, also on the Asaro river, is the site of the now celebrated ritual of the 'mudmen', in which the villagers engage with unfeigned relish and – perhaps – not a little inventiveness. The origins of this mud-dance are uncertain. In Kiminivi they say

it stems from a famous stratagem in their past. Hard-pressed by a stronger enemy, they decided that their only hope was to disguise themselves as ghosts. Covered in grey mud and wearing mud-masks to hide their human features, they advanced. It worked: the enemy panicked, ran, and were massacred. But according to a less romantic version, the mud-dance ritual was devised in order to win a tribal finery contest at the 1960 Agricultural Show at the nearby town of Goroka. The truth may be a mixture of the two.

This woman – in pidgin English a woman is a 'Mary' – has decorated her head with cassowary feathers.

A festival is one of the few occasions when pigs are slaughtered in the village. Later they will be roasted.

(Opposite) A Kiminivi man acts out the masquerade which – legend relates – panicked a stronger foe.

Dani Kurelu
New Guinea

Early morning in the courtyard
of a Dani compound. Smoke
from the cooking fires seeps
through the thatch to mingle
with low cloud.

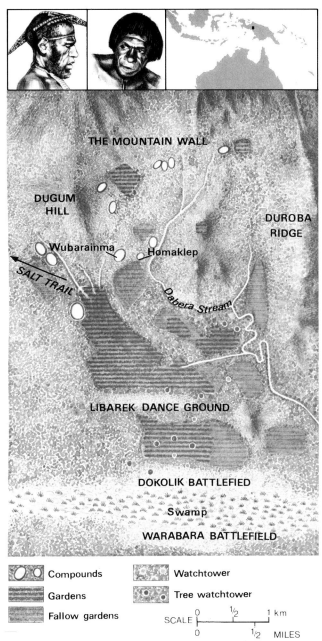

In the Snow Mountains of Irian Barat, the Baliem River vanishes underground to burst out of the mountain wall into the Grand Valley. It is 10 miles wide and 50 miles long and has a population of about 75,000 Dani-speaking people. Among Dani people are the Kurelu tribesmen. Within the valley most tribes are engaged in year round disputes and war with one another; often with their closest neighbors. By postulating a perpetual enemy the Kurelu – like their neighbors – derive a powerful sense of corporate identity. Battle is joined in the spirit of a sport where rules of combat are strictly observed. For the Dani a balance of casualties on

93

Dani people from the villages of Homaklep and Wubarainma normally fight at Dokolik and Warabara, and celebrate victories at Libarek.

each side is a satisfactory outcome.

In 1961 there was still one Dani tribe, the Kurelu, which had had little contact with the outside world. The Kurelu are a well-built people, varying in skin color from light brown to near black. A man's main article of dress is his penis sheath, an elongated gourd that often rises vertically to his shoulders, tied erect by a fiber thread round the chest. The sheaths are sometimes decorated with fur tassels, bands of woven fiber, or an elegant curl at the tip. They serve both as protection in battle and as a kind of fertility symbol. A bib of cowrie shells is a demonstration of wealth as well as fashion. A woman, once married, wears a loosely strung skirt of fiber coils woven by the man, while as a child she wore rushes. More efficient covering, worn even by little girls, is the series of overlapping woven nets hanging from a headband on the forehead. A woman's full nets may include a load of vegetables, a small pig, or a baby bouncing off its mother's hip.

Small net bags hung over the shoulders are used by old

men to carry their belongings. A young man pushes his tools into his arm bands, to keep his hands free to carry weapons – a spear of laurel or myrtle, or a four foot longbow cut from woodland rhododendron or laurel. The hardwood arrows, only slightly shorter than the bow, are unfeathered, which limits the accuracy of flight. A war arrowhead is barbed with flint chips, making it difficult to withdraw from the wound and the base of the point is carefully weakened so that head will snap off inside the body. Hunting arrows have knobbed, pronged heads. The other implements of the Dani are simple – digging sticks for the gardens, the highly effective cleft stick and rattan used for making fires, the ceremonial whisk of cassowary feathers or baton of egret feathers twirled in war, and the all-purpose stone axes and adzes.

The Kurelu tribe, living in a 30 square mile area in the northeast corner of the valley, take their name from Kurelu, the most important leader or *kain*. Leadership is not hereditary, but depends on a man's value in war, wealth or crafts and even then he earns not power but only the possibility of influence. The Dani are incorrigible individualists. A cowardly man, called *kepu*, will probably lose wives or pigs because he lacks the power to retaliate against aggressors, but will not be a social outcast, and may still have his head lice picked by the greatest *kain*. The Dani are polygamous and have as many wives as their wealth can support. The children have no close ties with their physical parents, and may spend most of their time with their indulgent *nami*, or godparent, who is usually their maternal uncle. All these relationships are fluid, as Dani base their lives on circumstances rather than rules.

When a young girl is about four, she puts on a loosely hung skirt. At about the age of six years a boy begins wearing the penis sheath, usually just a symbolic gourd dangling from his waist. Girls quickly learn to be useful but the young boys are given much more freedom for play. However, the play itself, throwing grass spears through hoops, maneuvering armies of seeds for war, or building miniature houses while watching the pigs, is preparation for adult life. None of the tribe's ceremonies is hidden from the children so they are quickly integrated into the Dani way of life.

The Kurelu territory is organised in the basic Dani pattern of villages which are dotted about the land and surrounded by 'gardens.' High watch-towers guard each territory from raids by their enemies. A warrior almost constantly perches 25 feet above the ground, gazing across the no-man's land. A village is divided into two or three enclosures called *sili*, each with a paling fence of split planks. Within the *sili* are a communal men's house and cooking house, a number of women's houses and as many pig shelters as there are pig owners. The men's house, a conical two-storey thatched hut about 15 feet in diameter, is shared by several men and young boys. The loft is used for sleeping and the ground floor, centered by a hearth, for the manufacture and storage of weapons.

A watchtower sentry looks out over no-man's land on guard against a raiding party from the enemy.

Away from the fighting an army masses prior to battle, shouting challenges to the enemy.

The number of women's huts varies according to the wealth of their husbands. An argumentative wife is often sent to the pig villages higher on the mountain for the sake of domestic peace.

On a day of peace, the men leave the village first; some to the watch towers, others to the gardens, and the women follow them to the fields. The Grand Valley, unlike the major part of the New Guinea Highlands, is highly cultivated in neat plots surrounded by irrigation ditches. Because of the temperate climate, a family will always have plots in all the various stages of development. The land is quickly leached of minerals and the gardens must often be moved. A man digs new ditches and breaks open the land with a large oarlike digging stick. After the plot is prepared, the women plant the sweet-potato spears – they are not only used to cultivate but also for self-defence.

Taro is grown in the ditches, cucumber in the gardens and bananas, mushrooms and toa (large succulent grasses) are gathered from the fields. Salt is collected in shredded banana bark from a saline pool in the northern Kurelu territory. The children take the pigs from the stalls, treat their rat bites and herd them to pasturage. These animals are used in financial exchanges and ceremonies. However, as their meat is the only substantial escape from vegetarianism, a need for a ceremony can be found if a man fancies roast pork. The Kurelu do not practise cannibalism, although they are aware that it occurs in the southern part of the Grand Valley.

The major activity of the Dani is war. It is caused by the need to revenge a murdered man so that his ghost may rest in peace. As the enemy, the neighboring tribe called the Wittaia, has the same reason, the cycle is never-ending. The score of fatalities should be even and a battle will often cease in the hope that the wounded will die off in equal proportions. If a tribe has too many ghosts to revenge, the people are troubled. A raiding party, of up to 100 men, creep through the underbush to kill any unwary man, woman or child. After the challenges to battle and a lapse of some hours, both sides recruit additional warriors, grease their bodies, put on their best headdresses and eat sweet potato. The old men gather to prepare for the wounded, the youths to observe and learn and the *kepu,* the cowards, to hover nervously in the background. About noon a group of thirty or so men charge in a feint attack on the enemy.

After an interchange of cat calls, laughed at by both sides, the war begins. Of perhaps 500 warriors, 100 will attack, racing towards the enemy bent almost double to protect the vulnerable parts of the body from the enemies' arrows. The more serious spear wounds are received in the man-to-man encounters which spring up on the front line. After about 15 minutes the groups retire with some warriors collecting arrows in their backs. 95

In the isolated Dani valley a
tribal battle reaches its climax.
One death is often sufficient to
satisfy honor.

Adorned with furs, mud, shells
and feathers the Dani shout
and sing to celebrate the death
of an opponent.

Dani Kurelu New Guinea

A wounded man is carried from the battlefield to be treated by the old men with leaves and herbs.

(Below) The funeral pyre awaits the corpse of a man killed in battle. Around it men and women join in mourning.

The corpse of a youth is displayed in a chair, decorated with cowrie belts and nets before being burnt.

The wounded either limp from the field or are carried on the shoulders of their friends to the rear, where the old men remove the arrows and bind the wounds with leaves. The war continues with constant replacements until the casualties are satisfactory, night has fallen, or it begins to rain.

If a man is badly wounded by a spear thrust, the Kurelu carry him back to his hut in the *sili*. Small cuts are made in his stomach to let the 'black blood' escape. A fetish of sugar cane with feathers inserted is waved over his head and then planted on the village patch to warn enemy ghosts that his spirit is protected. A man noted for cures blows into his ears to encourage the 'seed of singing,' the soul of the man, to fight the enemy spirits. If the man dies an intricate funeral ritual begins. The next full day the men and women of his village and clan gather to mourn in the *sili* yard before the dead man. A pig is cooked and gifts of cowrie belts and nets are presented, to be later distributed by the *kain*. The corpse is then carried to the waiting pyre and the spirit released to fly into enemy country to cause trouble. After a season the ghost returns to linger near the dead man's water calabash which will have been left by his brother under a tree near the frontier.

Returning to the village, the rest of the pig is eaten while a mutilation ritual is carried out. In this rite, two joints from the outer fingers of the left hands of little girls are cut off to honor the dead. If the mourning is particularly deep for an important man, a boy loses the top third of his ear. An old woman sits by the funeral fire, picking the bones from the ashes. She makes a small leaf bundle of these last remains of the dead man and adds the severed fingers. It is then buried outside the village.

Every few years, when the people are rich in pigs and the ghosts do not seek revenge, Kurelu, the chief, will call for a *mauwe,* a week long festival. Hundreds of pigs are slaughtered, no war is fought, no work is done, buildings and friendships are mended. The clans' holy stones, smooth flat green or black stones passed down from the ancestors, are taken out of their lead packages and rubbed with fresh pig grease. But the main business of the *mauwe* is the initiation of the boys and girls into the tribe followed by the marriage of the eligible girls. As no girl is so ugly or poor that some man will not take her on as an additional wife, spinsterhood is unknown. It may take several years to accumulate enough wealth to repeat such an extravagant festival.

According to the Kurelu, their history is short. The father's father of the present generation, a man called Nopu, came from the mountains with his wife and a great bundle of living things. Nopu's children opened the bundle against his wishes, releasing the mosquitoes and snakes to the world. As no artefacts survive to be dated by the anthropologist, this legend is as good an account as any. It has survived the arrival of missionaries and government officials and even the initiation of the Kurelu into the 1971 Indonesian elections.

Trobriand Islanders

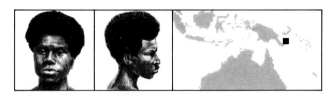

TUMA I.

Kaibola

BOYOWA

Koma

Omarakana

Moligilagi

Losuia

Olivelevi

KAILEUNA I.

Kavatari

KITAVA I.

Sinaketa

TROBRIAND ISLANDS

KIRIWINA ISLANDS

VAKUTA I.

SCALE
0 10 20 30 40 km
0 10 20 30 MILES

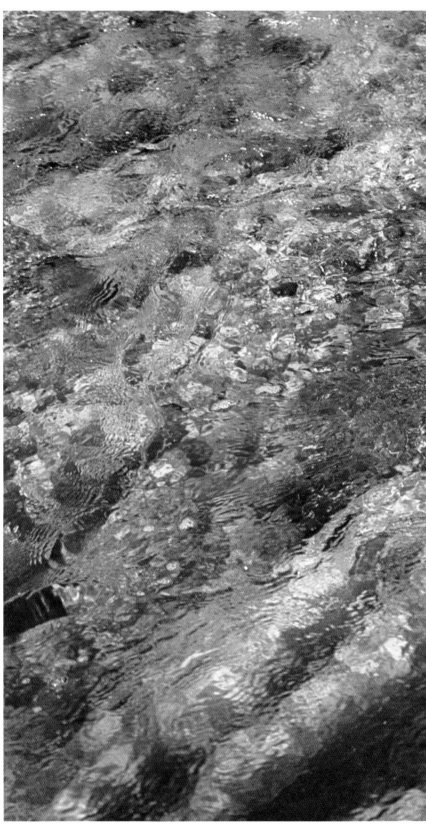

The canoe-fishermen of the Trobriand islands have come to exemplify what novelists and film-makers mean by 'South Sea Islanders.' The freedom with which Trobriand adolescents exchange sexual partners, the fidelity they display towards their life-long marital partners, the beauty of the people and of their island homeland, the picturesque nature of their fishing and their uniquely complex system of exchange – all have made the Trobriand Islands the Eden of the Western Pacific. Even allowing for romantic exaggeration, Trobriand society is remarkably attractive. Despite the impact of the European, much remains of Trobriander traditional ways. Fifty years ago, the Trobrianders were first brought to the attention of the world, when Bronislaw Malinowski first visited them and wrote of them in his book *Argonauts of the Western Pacific*. Since then they have received much attention from anthropologists.

Their coral islands are covered with rich soil, well suited to the cultivation of yams and taro. Off the main island, Boyowa, a huge shallow lagoon teems with fish.

101

Trobriand children learn to
swim at an early age. Fishing
and canoeing will take up a
large part of their adult life.

Trobriand Islanders

Shell necklaces and bracelets indicate the high rank of this Trobriand islander. Because of his status he may also have more than one wife.

A Trobriand mother carries food back from her garden leaving it in the care of the men who will perform magical rites and make it fertile.

Despite the simplicity of their tools the islanders are efficient, industrious cultivators and expert fishermen, and apart from the need to import stone and clay have managed to remain fairly self-sufficient. Not all villages on Boyowa have equal access to the sea, and traditionally the exchange of surplus fish from the coastal villages has always been an important economic and ceremonial institution. Each village is surrounded by its own territory, and has a water-hole, fruit trees and palm groves. The plan is of two concentric rings of houses; an inner ring of yam storehouses and an outer ring of dwelling huts. The central area, set aside for dances and feasts, is also the traditional burial ground. The village usually consists of less than a hundred persons, belonging to a variety of clans and sub-clans.

Every person belongs to one of four clans, and, since the Trobrianders believe in reincarnation, an individual *never* loses his clan identity. The Trobriand origin myth tells of the appearance on earth of the four spirit ancestors, while other myths record the emergence of sub-clans, establishing their claims to particular areas of land. Membership of a clan and sub-clan is determined by one's mother, for descent is reckoned matrilineally.

Chiefly rank is accorded to all men of certain sub-clans. One of these sub-clans is the Tabalu, whose members enjoy a special prestige. They are addressed by chiefly title, wear insignia of shells and take more than one wife. But they are also obliged to observe certain dietary taboos, and the higher the rank the more stringent these are. Sub-clans of high rank are also credited with the possession of dangerous magical powers – for example, the Tabalu hold potent weather magic which can bring

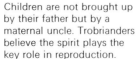
Children are not brought up by their father but by a maternal uncle. Trobrianders believe the spirit plays the key role in reproduction.

In outrigger canoes Trobriand
men travel hundreds of miles
on *kula* exchange expeditions.
An exchange partnership is a
lifelong affair.

The annual yam harvest is being stored in elaborately decorated yam houses. Interlacing logs allow air to circulate freely.

famine or prosperity to the whole of Boyowa.

The leader or chief of the village is generally the oldest able-bodied male of the dominant sub-clan. Over and above these local leaders there is no centralized authority, no administrative or governmental machinery; in short, nothing resembling a state. Social control is informal, disputes being settled by the relatives and friends of those involved. Appeal can be made to public opinion, and aggrieved parties can challenge each other to competitive yam displays, or cricket matches. It is the collective responsibility of the sub-clan to take reprisals or settle compensation where necessary. The chief's power to punish is principally ritualistic: he is believed to command destructive weather magic and can employ sorcerers to afflict with sickness and death those who challenge his authority.

Individual households comprise a married couple and their young children, living among the husband's maternal kinsmen in the village owned by his sub-clan. Daughters remain in the parental household until they marry; sons leave their parents earlier and move to a village house which they share with other boys of their age. Adolescents of both sexes enjoy a life of untrammelled sexual freedom. During this time, however, relationships are established which lead to marriage, and once married a couple are expected to be faithful to one another. Marriage requires the consent of both parties' parents and is by a series of presents which pass between the two families. The groom then takes his bride to dwell in the village of his maternal kinsmen, where he assumes his rights.

Legally speaking, a father is not a kinsman to his children but a stranger; he is just their mother's husband, following the Trobriand view that all inheritance of blood, property, power and spirit pass from the mother. Their children's real guardian is their mother's brother. Trobrianders actually deny the father's role in procreation. Whether or not the Trobrianders are 'ignorant of physiological paternity' has been much debated. According to Trobriand belief, the father's role is limited to 'opening the way' for the entry of a spirit child. This is nurtured by the mother's blood during pregnancy. A human being, then, is composed entirely of maternal substance – substance he shares with his mother's kinsmen.

An important duty of every married man is his annual harvest gift of yams (about half of his crop) – which he must make to the household of his sister. He is, after all, the guardian of her children. His wife, of course, will be the beneficiary of a similar household gift from her brother. Men of rank, notably chiefs, can take more than one wife. It is through their position as heads of large polygymous households that Trobriand chiefs become wealthy and powerful. With the wives coming from many villages, the unions are often important community alliances. The annual harvest gifts which the chief

receives from his wives' kinsmen constitute a kind of

The decorative carving on the prow of an outrigger canoe illustrates the importance the islanders attach to their ocean-going sailing craft.

(Center) Trobriand canoes are built from hollowed out logs. Before they can be considered seaworthy many magical rites must be performed.

Between the yam stores and the dwellings the daily chores of life take place. Here a woman prepares a meal cooked in a large clay pot.

tribute. The chiefly 'brother-in-law' then uses his wealth to sponsor communal enterprises – warfare, feasts and ceremonies, and *kula* expeditions.

The *kula* trading network involves ceremonial exchanges over vast areas of sea both within the Trobriands and between other neighboring islands. Around a wide ring of islands, a thousand miles by sea-going canoe, shell valuables of two kinds are passed from hand to hand. Red shell necklaces move in a clockwise direction, while white shell bracelets move anticlockwise. The necklaces are manufactured among the islands of the south, and the bracelets are produced in the Trobriands. In every community the men of the *kula* ring receive the valuables, hold them for a short time, then pass them on to life-long exchange partners. In return they receive valuables of the opposite class. The rule 'once in the *kula*, always in the *kula*' applies both to partnerships and valuables. As the valuables circulate around the ring, they acquire a reputation. They are named, and stories told about them and the people who have owned them.

Overseas *kula* expeditions entail elaborate preparation, for island neighbors are rarely bound by the same customs. To avert hostility, magic is important. Rites are performed over the sea-going canoe when it is built to make it safe, swift and lucky. During voyages, magic is used to counter inclement weather and 'flying witches.' And when the destination is reached it is used again to woo and soften the hosts so that they will be eager to part with their valuables.

To enter the *kula* a young man must be acquainted with the magic spells and own one valuable shell. He must also be familiar with the etiquette of this fraternal exchange in which haggling is entirely absent. The partnership is clinched by the presentation of the valuable; the recipient undertakes to make a return gift of the other type at a later date. All transactions are sealed by ceremonies which express ideals of honorable gift-giving and mutual trust. This ethic of friendship or quasi-kinship precludes unscrupulous dealing among men who might otherwise have been hostile strangers. The *kula* has traditionally helped to establish a 'peace of the market' for trade in vital commodities, particularly stone and pottery.

'Civilization' has now come, bringing schools, a hospital and a local government council to the Trobriands. Despite these changes much of the indigenous culture survives. The standard of living remains the same, traditional dress is still worn and villages are organized on the same lines as before. The *kula* is maintained, although government or mission boats are sometimes used instead of canoes. But now that goods can be bought for cash at a local store the bartering trade is rapidly declining. Yet still today the otherwise functionless *kula* articles are exchanged, for they are the traditional symbols of prestige and lend a sense of community to the scattered islanders.

The Peoples of Melanesia

Melanesia – 'the islands of the Blacks' – is a great crescent of islands stretching south-eastwards from New Guinea down through the Solomon Islands to the New Hebrides and New Caledonia. Some of the islands are mere coral atolls, but in general they are much larger than the Polynesian Islands to the east. In the dense Melanesian rain forest and rugged mountains, live the last people to remain untouched by European civilisation. Parts of New Guinea have still never been mapped.

Melanesia is politically divided. Australia administers the eastern half of New Guinea, which includes Papua, while Indonesia has the western half. The Solomons are British, New Caledonia is French. Britain and France jointly rule the New Hebrides. But despite the often haphazardly drawn boundaries, Melanesia maintains its ethnic unity. Its frizzy-haired people are much darker than the Polynesians and Indonesians, whose society is more sophisticated. Melanesian languages form a distinct group. The tribes are small, and often cut off completely from the outside world. Except in New Caledonia, there are no chiefs, councils of elders or other features of centralized society. Melanesians mainly grow root-crops, unlike the neighbouring Indonesians who prefer seed-crops or the Aborigines who are traditionally hunters and gatherers.

However, Melanesians are not the only people on the islands. Polynesians, Micronesians, Chinese and Europeans have all moved in over the years. The first inhabitants of the islands were probably negroid peoples who migrated *en masse* through South-East Asia down to New Guinea about 20,000 years ago and gradually continued down the island crescent. Scattered groups of light-skinned Polynesians and Micronesians sailed over in the last 1,000 years and settled along the shores. Some of the Solomon Islanders originated from as far away as the Gilbert and Ellice Islands 1,000 miles to the north-east. The Melanesians gradually retired into the inhospitable mountains or onto the myriad islands nearby. The highland tribes were continually at war. Some, like the Namba on Malekula Island in the New Hebrides, are still hostile and resent intruders.

These migrations have produced people of varying looks. Those from the coastal and swampy regions are taller with finer features than the inland mountain peoples. These are shorter, stockier and more negroid: some resemble pygmies. Many people are pot-bellied, because of the starchy diet of *taro*, breadfruit and sweet potatoes. Along the coasts, fish are eaten. Pigs are commonly kept throughout the islands and are usually eaten only at ceremonial feasts. In a few tribes, pork is forbidden to the women, who are generally treated as inferior. Wives are often beaten, and sexual relations are sometimes violent.

Captain Cook named and charted the New Hebrides in 1774, but the possibilities for trade were first explored after 1800. The Solomons were ransacked by 'black-birders' looking for cheap labor for the Queensland plantations. Gold, tortoiseshell and pearls were later found. In the New Hebrides, copra-trading began. New Caledonia became a French penal colony, after a French expedition there was massacred. The convicts were freed when traders arrived to exploit iron, nickel, chromium, manganese, copper and gold. Populations in the New Hebrides and the Solomons dwindled sharply because of heavy recruitment of labor, and punitive slaughter. Malaria and dysentery were already widespread, but Europeans brought measles, whooping-cough, tuberculosis, venereal diseases and influenza – all major killers.

Westerners have seen Melanesians in different lights. Early settlers told of savagery and barbarism. Some travelers described a land of beauty and exotic living, while others viewed the Melanesian as a benign layabout paddling aimlessly around in a canoe. Many explorers have been horrified by reports of cannibalism, which existed in many parts of Melanesia. Two quite opposed ideas explain the eating of man by man. Some isolated tribes have so strong a sense of self-identity that *all* outsiders are considered animals: the flesh of a baby from a different tribe is just another chunk of game-food. On the other hand, some cannibals eat both the enemy and respected relatives in order to inherit their admired qualities.

Reports and opinions on the Melanesian life-style vary. What is certain, however, is the traumatic effect of the European arrival on the Melanesian populace. The trauma is exemplified by the bizarre 'cargo cult' which is widespread throughout most of the islands. Melanesians believe that all material things are sent by the spirits. Seeing that the Europeans had many wonderful goods, the Melanesians were eager to worship the same spirits as the Europeans. Early Christian missionaries thus met with great success; and the newly converted then expected to receive valuable treasures too.

The story of the Israelites in Egypt receiving manna from heaven strengthened this conviction, and platforms were built to catch the 'manna'. The advent of aeroplanes still further reinforced the faith of the Melanesians. But when neither manna nor cargo arrived, the Melanesians were left bewildered and disappointed. They said the priests were deliberately withholding some vital secret. Perhaps they had torn out the Bible's crucial pages, containing the magic cargo-producing formula. Even today, many Melanesians still embrace the cargo cults, in the hope that the treasure will arrive. The Melanesians have all been deeply disturbed by a situation they do not understand. The cargo cults represent an attempt to fit an unknown phenomenon into their own religious world-view. There are variations in the cults – but they all reflect the drastic effects of an alien people imposing themselves on an indigenous society.

NEW GUINEA

AUSTRA

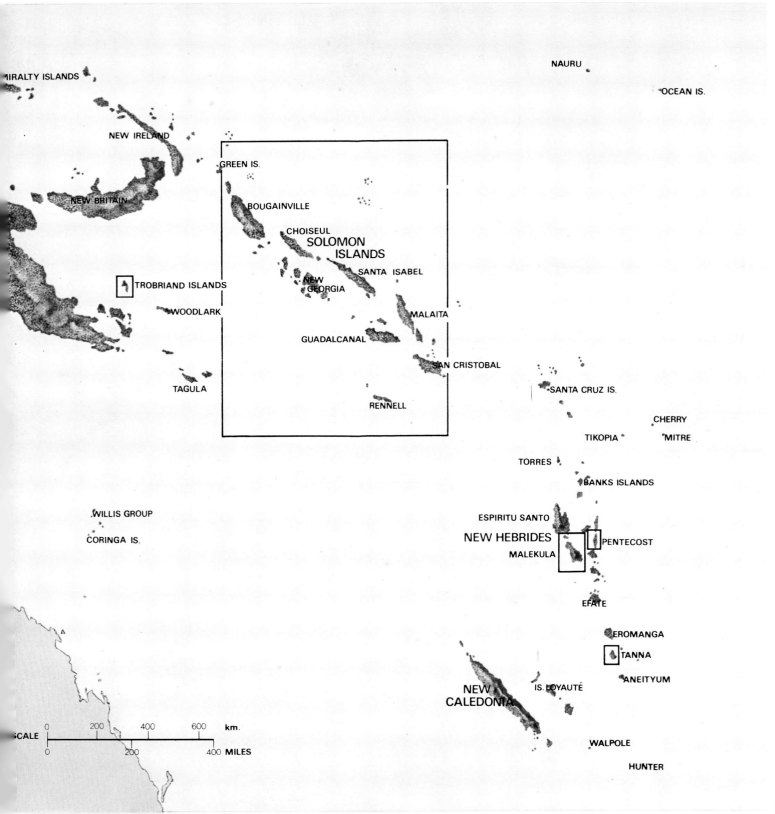

Melanesians spread through these islands some 20,000 years ago. Rectangles show areas of peoples in this volume.

NAURU

OCEAN IS.

MIRALTY ISLANDS

NEW IRELAND

GREEN IS.

NEW BRITAIN

BOUGAINVILLE

CHOISEUL

SOLOMON
ISLANDS

SANTA ISABEL

TROBRIAND ISLANDS

NEW
GEORGIA

WOODLARK

MALAITA

TAGULA

GUADALCANAL

SAN CRISTOBAL

RENNELL

SANTA CRUZ IS.

CHERRY

TIKOPIA

MITRE

TORRES

BANKS ISLANDS

WILLIS GROUP

ESPIRITU SANTO

CORINGA IS.

NEW HEBRIDES

PENTECOST

MALEKULA

EFATE

EROMANGA

TANNA

ANEITYUM

NEW
CALEDONIA

IS. LOYAUTÉ

SCALE

| 0 | 200 | 400 | 600 | km. |

WALPOLE

| 0 | 200 | 400 | MILES |

HUNTER

107

Solomon Islanders
Melanesia

108

Melanesian blood — indicated
by this fine head of frizzy hair
and negroid features —
predominates among the
Solomon Islanders.

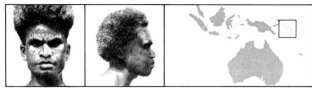

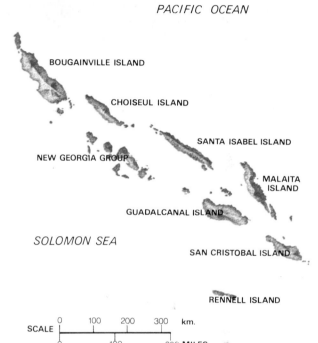

PACIFIC OCEAN

BOUGAINVILLE ISLAND

CHOISEUL ISLAND

SANTA ISABEL ISLAND

NEW GEORGIA GROUP

MALAITA
ISLAND

GUADALCANAL ISLAND

SOLOMON SEA

SAN CRISTOBAL ISLAND

RENNELL ISLAND

SCALE

0   100   200   300   km.

0   100   200 MILES

The arrival of the bonito (striped tunnies) off the coral islands of the Solomon group is an event that has an almost religious significance for the islanders. The bonito come during a single season of the year, but the exact time of their arrival is unpredictable. At first great flocks of birds appear, clustering above the sea and feeding off the multitude of other fish that accompany the bonito. With the coming of the birds, the Solomon Islanders know that their waiting has been rewarded.

Sacred canoes are brought out from their houses and launched into the sea to race out for the fishing. There will be plenty to eat for the islanders for the bonito is highly prized as a food. But there will also be much danger; the great shoals of fish also attract the sharks. Grey fins are seen circling the schools of bonito as the men use long lines of nets to trap the fish. This is then followed by the spear throwing in which the huge tunnies are killed. Yet as the men lean out of their canoes to pull the fish in or regain a spear, the sharks often attack. Their prey is any living thing – which can easily be the arm of a fisherman.

109

The bonito disappear almost as rapidly and mysteriously as they come. Yet to have come at all is a good omen for the islanders. The fickleness of the bonito and the viciousness of the sharks both seem to reflect the qualities of the islanders' own gods, whose whim sends them this food. If the bonito appear regularly it is taken as a sign that all is well between the islanders and their gods. Should the fish not appear it is a sign that the gods are angry.

Bonito fishing has such importance for the Solomon Islanders that even the houses in which the sacred canoes are stored are regarded as shrines where the community can pay its respects to the deities. Every boy in the Eastern Solomon Islands must go through a ritual initiation to introduce him to the mysteries of bonito fishing. This begins when a group of young men go out to meet the canoes bringing in a successful catch. Each boy is taken into a canoe where he embraces one of the great fish, and then comes ashore with the bonito as though it were his own. The supernatural qualities of the fish are passed on to the boy by his drinking of a few drops of its blood. The boys then live for up to two years in the canoe house – away from women and all normal life of the community.

When the boys return to village life there is a celebration in which they dress in adult finery and parade on an elaborate platform before the rest of the community. A feast is held to celebrate their return, for they are now regarded as men. In their time in the canoe house they have lost any need for their mothers and are thus prepared for the work of men – the great fishing.

Excavations during the last few years have indicated that the small island of Santa Ana has been occupied by man at least since A.D. 140. Cave floors have revealed flint-like blades and volcanic stones damaged by domestic fires. There has also been found a type of coarse pottery unknown on the island today. It indicates that a thousand years ago the Eastern Solomon Islanders gave up making pottery. It is something for which there is no explanation.

On the larger island of Guadalcanal, excavations in the Poha Valley, a few miles from the town of Honiara, have revealed more gruesome relics of the past. The upper level of the site contained thousands of American ·45 bullets, Japanese cartridge cases and an Oriental skeleton. Digging down brought to light artifacts of varying ages and, 12 feet beneath the surface, there was charcoal. Radio-carbon dating showed it to be of a period around 970 B.C. Evidently there had been 3,000 years of occupation on the island.

The lives of the Solomon Islanders continued almost unchanged until World War II. They kept their stone-age tools and mysteriously lost their ceramic art. A benevolent British colonial rule was established in the late 19th century. Then came the violent Japanese invasion. There followed desperate fighting between the Japanese and the

Three women of the Solomon Islands exemplify the mixed origins of these Pacific peoples, the paler skins suggesting a mixture of various strains.

(Below center) Family life among the Islanders is remarkable for the close contact that is maintained between father and children.

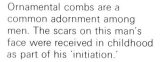

Ornamental combs are a common adornment among men. The scars on this man's face were received in childhood as part of his 'initiation.'

This village in the Lav lagoon, Malaita, is built up on tiny islands of coral rock. Such villages off-shore were safer from attack by inland tribes.

(Over page) Built on piles, a man's house in the Lav lagoon off Malaita is accessible both by a structure of poles and by canoe.

Fishermen surround shoals of fish with nets dropped from their canoes. With the fish trapped, the men use spears to bring in their catch.

Americans – fighting that seemed both horrifying and spectacular to the islanders. The Americans' victory meant the establishment of a vast military complex where thousands of the islanders were employed.

Unthought of wealth flooded in on the islanders; pickings from the junk heaps and surplus stores. It was a revelation, an indication of the overwhelming material bounty of Western civilization. Although the British eventually returned, things could never be the same after the islanders had known the Americans' profligate generosity.

A new cult, allied to a political movement, spread throughout the Solomon Islands between the years of 1944 and 1953. Its leader was a visionary who demanded a new social order that would bring wealth for all and complete independence from the British. It was called Marching Rule and started on Malaita, then the most populated of the islands. From there it spread westward to Santa Isabel and south to Guadalcanal. When the cult was at its height natives from the other islands often travelled by canoe to Malaita where they attended mass meetings and eagerly listened to speeches from their leaders. Then, curiously, there came a great change.

A man named Moro had a vision concerning the origins of his island. The vision was incorporated into a charter for a socio-religious movement which aimed at establishing a political organization with Moro at its head. Co-operative ventures were inspired to raise the standard of living of all members. Soon the movement had been renamed the Moro Custom Company and had earned the attention of the Government.

Guadalcanal, where Moro had his original vision, is 90 miles long and 30 miles across. Rugged mountains reach to 7,000 feet and drop off sharply to the southern coast. During the War it was across the northern plains that the great battle for the island had been fought. There it is relatively dry for half the year, but the south is hit by trade winds and heavily pounded by the sea. And here saw the first determined attempt by the Government to boost the economy of the islanders. They sent agricultural technicians to increase copra production and see to the planting of larger areas with coconut trees. But it was not enough to stem the growth of the Custom Company. Moro and his supporters continued to gain new recruits and collect larger funds of money – in local shell currency and Australian notes – with which to fortify the organization.

Moro's vision had come when he was taken ill on a fishing trip. During the crisis of his illness he became unconscious and at one point all signs of breathing ceased. Arrangements were made for his funeral and pigs were sought for a feast. Then he started to breathe again. Later he talked excitedly about a vision he had had, though at first people thought him mad. 'I saw a bird,' he said, 'but it was a man who instructed me to do all the things he told me . . . "Everything in this land is yours and 111

the sea belongs to you. You must start a company to make money. All the things that are yours should be used".'

Guadalcanal is called Isatabu by Moro and his followers. In the headquarters of the movement, the village of Makaruka, the company has built a Custom House which is both the shrine and the treasury of the organization. On the wall of the house a bird is painted, its wings spread and its head in profile. This represents the bird Moro saw in his vision. Inside the house there are carvings of a hawk with a fish in its beak. This symbolizes the creation of Isatabu and figures of dogs represent the stage in its creation when there were no humans. Stored on the shelves are baskets of shell currency and objects that have a special meaning in the mythical history of the island.

Moro's Custom Company is one reaction to the meeting of Western civilization with a primitive culture. The effects seem strange in this case, but other effects are more easily understood and predictable. Many of the indigenous art forms have been eroded or are currently being discarded. Though the practice of some art continues in some communities, it no longer flourishes as it did fifty years ago. With the Pacific, and its islands, increasingly coming under the spell and influence of the modern world, old cultures die and are soon forgotten.

Two sorts of objects are still representative of local carving. One is of a male figure with a pig-like snout; the other is a composition of birds or fish, carved as the end of an oval bowl. The figures of men are religious icons that were traditionally fixed to large canoes, like those used for bonito fishing. The bowls are for ritual offerings to the deities. But these two art forms come from different parts of the Solomon Islands: the carved figures from the Western Islands and the bowls from the Eastern. And in these two areas the people have both distinct languages and different cultures.

Styles of carving throughout the islands are deeply personal. Some carvers employ apprenticed assistants to finish the work once the design and form has been decided on. Others will not allow anyone else to do even the finishing – which is executed with a small adze, pumice stone or scrapers of broken glass. Until 75 years ago blades of stone and shell were used for almost all the work on a carving. Even today the artists' tools remain simple. Adzes of scrap iron, ground down to the correct shape on hard, volcanic rock, are now the standard tools. A sharp nail serves as a drill, and a sharpened screwdriver or flattened spike as the chisel or gouge. For whittling down the wood most carvers use only an old, well-worn table knife.

Sculptures are normally painted. All the colors are natural, the black coming from powdered charcoal mixed with the sap of a tree. The white is from lime, obtained by burning the coral rock of the coast; and the 'terra cotta' from the red earth. Many of the sacred canoes and fine bowls are inlaid with shell, including mother of pearl, cut

from the thin nautilus shells which drift ashore. Most men are able to build the utility canoes – certainly the most suitable vessel for use near the jagged coral shores of the islands – but it is left to the expert to construct the larger bonito or trading canoes. Usually it becomes a group effort in which many men provide their various talents – and the result is a fine, sea-worthy and ornamented canoe.

A man who can build a good house and a sound general purpose canoe, who can carve and perform delicate operations in which geometric patterns are cut into children's faces as marks of their social identity, is considered a 'talented man.' To achieve this status he must be skilled in all the arts – in a survey of 1,500 men living in Star Harbor, Santa Ana and Santa Cantalina, no more than ten were rated as 'talented.' A similar rating is used for women who must possess the arts of plaiting fans, baskets and mats as well as the complex tattooing which is traditionally applied for cosmetic reasons.

Few personal ornaments are worn by the Solomon Islanders, except on ceremonial occasions. Most artistic are the nose pendants worn by the men, and the ear decorations ground from shells. The delicacy of the carving on a person's ornaments indicates his or her social status. For the women the ornaments are almost functional. They wear strings of shell-money about their arms and legs, around the waist and across the shoulders. Thus they are rarely seen on ritual occasions without their wealth.

Houses and their furnishings are normally left unornamented, but objects designed for public occasions and display are decorated with impressive carvings. The food bowls have their carved ends which serve both to please the eye, demonstrate the family's talents and identify the bowls during public feasts. On Santa Ana, each man has a carved ritual pole used for private ceremonies with his supernatural guide. In other places a carved bowl is used for a similar purpose, but inlaid with much shell.

During these rituals each worshipper eats in communion with his god – but there are other occasions when the worshippers take communion together as a congregation. These are ceremonies in which commemorative rites for the dead are also held and their focal place is the canoe house. And here, more than anywhere, the best of the islanders' aesthetic skills are lavished. Carvings depict mythical, religious and ritual events with complex compositions of figures. It is a place in which the secular domain of man intersects the sacred domain of the gods.

For the current generation of Solomon Islanders there remains the problem of adjusting this ritual way of life to increasing European influence. Both cultural and economic styles are inexorably undermined by contact with a modern, unritualistic world – the Moro Custom Company movement is one, largely secular, response to the problem. Another is the gradual abandoning of beautiful and traditional art forms.

A woman uses a locally devised pump drill to bore a shell for stringing. After smoothing, the shell will have become shell-money.

A diver brings up a fish killed by the blast from a Japanese salvage operation. Traditional fishing methods involve nets and spears.

The 'market chief' awaits the arrival of the throng of women who will buy and sell fish and garden produce. Bargaining is brisk and often heated.

Solomon Islanders set out on a dawn fishing expedition — this time with small nets for small fish, which will be shared out equally among participants.

Tannese
New Hebrides

SCALE

The arrival of American troops on the Western Pacific Islands during World War II brought to the islanders a wealth they had not known before. The endless flood of supplies and the generosity with which they were distributed, overwhelmed and mystified the islanders. None of this wealth was seen to be made on the spot; it all came in crates from the holds of ships and aircraft. The people of the islands neither understood the source of such wealth, nor the conditions necessary to obtain it. In effect it enhanced a belief in a 'cargo cult' by which adherence to the European, in particular to his Christian teachings, would somehow cause such wealth to come naturally to the islanders.

For the people of Tanna in the New Hebrides the cargo cult was headed by a mythical being known as John Frum. He differed from the other white men in knowing the Tannese dialects and customs, and it was to the islanders that he owed his allegiance. The John Frum cult came to official notice in 1939. Throughout the 3,000 miles range

117

Tannese pray to the cross at
the beginning of the annual
John Frum celebrations. The
red cross is derived either
from the American Red Cross
or from Christianity.

A Tannese gazes into the volcanic crater of Mt. Yasur where an army of 20,000 strong is ready to greet the cargo millennium.

On ceremonial ground Tannese boys play with a calf. When *kava* is being prepared and drunk the ground is forbidden to all women.

of the Melanesian Islands, from New Guinea to the New Hebrides, cargo cults exist, often headed by supernatural creations like John Frum. Christianity came to all the islands through missionaries, and with it an undermining of traditional beliefs. The missionaries also brought the first inexplicable cargoes and wonderful implements; to the natives these things quickly became fruits of the new religion. Later disillusion with Christianity set in – the cargo itself then became the object of worship.

First contact was in 1774 with Captain Cook's second voyage. In the first half of the nineteenth century relations between the intruding Europeans and the Tannese were transitory. Whalers and merchants traded alcohol, firearms and trinkets for such things as sea slugs, sandalwood and coconuts. Labor recruiters took the Tannese, sometimes by force, to work on sugar plantations in Queensland and Fiji. The first missionaries helped stop these 'press-gangs' while at the same time attacking the traditional practices of internecine fighting, the drinking of *kava* (a narcotic drink made from the roots of the Piper Methysticum bush) and the use of prostitutes for the sexual initiation of young men. In the eyes of the islanders the missionaries were wealthy men who could give away cloth and tools at their leisure.

Frequently the new religion was accepted merely because of its association with the wealth of the white men. And there was too an old legend which seemed to support this association. The Deity Kilibob, revered in New Guinea in the early twentieth century, had according to Lawrence's accounts in *Road Belong Cargo*, a vessel which he stocked with white men, black men, native artifacts, food plants and European cargo. At various stops along the coast Kilibob put a black man ashore giving him a choice of goods from the ship. Invariably the black man rejected the European goods. After all the black men had been deposited, Kilibob went to another country, where he left the white men with the European cargo. To them he also taught the proper rituals for obtaining similar goods.

By 1930 the rule of law in Tanna had become confused

by competition among the sectarian churches. A French District Agent had been sent to balance the influence of the Anglo-Saxon Presbyterian Church. A new alternative was presented by the arrival of the Seventh Day Adventists. Whole communities of converts, old opponents of the Presbyterians, joined the Adventist mission. Others simply left Christianity to return to traditional practices where *kava* was drunk as a way to contact spirits and supernatural beings.

Some natives claim that John Frum first made his 'appearance' in the early 1930s. But the movement only surfaced in 1940. The population at that time was almost 6,000 of which 60 per cent were Presbyterians, 30 per cent non-Christian, and the remaining were mostly Adventists or Roman Catholics. Reports were heard of a supernatural being, John Frum, was was promising a millennium with all the material goods the natives desired. The movement spread throughout Tanna and most of the missions became deserted.

Kava drinking became a daily occurrence and traditional dancing was resumed. European money was spent quickly because it was rumored that soon it would be useless. Hamlets that had been deserted by a shift to artificial villages (created for administrative ease) became reoccupied. Nicol, the District Agent, who had a reputation for favoring the Presbyterian sect, jailed or exiled some of those known to be leaders and tied to a tree the man whom he had thought impersonated John Frum. Unfortunately this man had only given himself up to stifle the inquiry; the true impersonator remained free.

The arrival of American troops in Tanna was said to be the work of John Frum. A thousand of the islanders volunteered to work for the Americans but the war years were followed by disappointment. John Frum's promises failed to materialize and there were new repressions on the part of the Anglo-French Condominium government. More leaders were jailed and exiled and some of the Tannese drifted back to their old allegiances at the missions. Yet the cult was far from dead.

Estimates of the number of cargo cult adherents vary

Crosses, the model of an
American bomber, and a
representation of John Frum
himself are clustered in a
place of worship.

Although light airplanes of Air
Melanesia visit Tanna Island
regularly, belief in a 'millennium'
brought by a massive descent
of cargo-laden aircraft remains.

119

A Tannese youth views the
cross of the mythical John
Frum in a sacred area on the
Yasur volcano overlooking
Lake Siwi.

A John Frum worshipper drinks *kava* – a mild narcotic – daily. Heightened sensibility leads to possible communication with spirits.

(Below center) A worshipper sprays the air with the last of the *kava* to seek the aid of John Frum, who is to bring miraculous cargoes of gifts.

Both the origin and markings of this 3 foot wooden symbol of the Kastom segment of the John Frum movement are keys to the after-life.

Pan flutes are usually played after circumcision. When the flutes sound, women must move away so that they do not see the boys.

considerably. A small proportion, perhaps 5 per cent, believe John Frum's millennium to be close at hand – but as many as 99 per cent believe they will eventually be rewarded for their belief in John Frum. In this way the cult can best be understood as a socio-religious movement. Just as in Western societies, there are both devout worshippers in a church, who are convinced of heaven and hell, and others who see churchgoing as a kind of insurance against the unforeseen. Seen thus the cargo cult is less a peculiar phenomenon than a response to an uncertain and changing world. The Tannese had neither the experience nor the abilities to obtain wealth like that belonging to visiting Westerners – instead they turned to another source, a mystical being who would provide if only they had faith in him. And still today there remains the awe with which the islanders regard white man's wealth.

It must not be assumed, however, that these John Frum followers form a uniform whole obeying a strict

Sudden American military presence in World War II amazingly reinforced the John Frum religious fantasy. Relics of the war are venerated.

After a circumcision ceremony, *laplap* – puddings made from taro, yams or bananas – and *kava*, a fermented root liquid – are distributed.

hierarchy of leaders. As in any movement schisms and fragmentations occur when promises are not realized and this is certainly the case in the Tanna cargo cult. In pre-contact times quarrels and rivalries kept the island in a state of constant warfare. Through force and persuasion the Europeans stopped the outright fighting but institutions capable of eliminating the causes of the underlying animosities were never created. In the first exalted sweep of the John Frum movement such things were set aside; but rivalries soon crept back.

In the south-west of the island the Tannese maintain that only a complete return to traditional ways will bring about the golden era promised by John Frum. They concede that a number of modern tools, such as axes and machetes, should be retained as these have become indispensable to their agriculture; but many of these same farmers have also put on leaf penis-wrappers again. This adornment is the most blatant symbolic defiance of westernization.

Perhaps the most interesting form of the cult exists at the village of Ipekel in Sulfur Bay. The nearby Yasur volcano is quite accessible and often visited by tourists. The Tannese consider the volcano to be under their sphere of influence; and the stones strewn about its crater to be a magical source of wisdom. Legend says that the white man drew his superior wisdom from stolen Yasur stones. The missionaries, as though confirming this, took the stones away. Now John Frum has returned them and no tourist is allowed to visit the crater except under the watchful eye of a guide.

The volcano is also important to the natives because they believe that John Frum has an army of 20,000 men inside the crater. This army is ready to come out when the Americans return with all the good things. Next to the volcano is an ash plain. It is kept in a state of readiness for the longed-for American planes. To the leaders of this cult at Sulfur Bay John Frum is supposed to have revealed all his rules. Many are assimilated from Christianity; strict injunctions against swearing, stealing and adultery. Huts must be kept clean at all times and Friday is to be substituted for Sunday as the day of rest. No cooperation is to be given to the Condominium administration and the symbol of the movement is to be a red cross. Some Tannese interpret this as the blood covered cross of Christ while a European resident says it is merely the red cross from a field jacket given to a leader by an American soldier.

One particular leader of this cult was baptized at birth and had all his early schooling from the Presbyterian church. Later he joined the Seventh Day Adventists. After their additional schooling he joined the Condominium Police and in five years rose to the rank of sergeant. He became an Adventist missionary of the island of Malekula, attempting to convert the non-Christians. When he returned to Tanna the John Frum movement was just beginning. Soon he had abandoned all his training to become a leader of the cult. He was jailed and exiled and believes he was only freed to return to Tanna because of intervention on the part of the Americans. Now he is one of the three main leaders of the Sulfur Bay cult and he asks any visiting American for news regarding John Frum's influence in the U.S.

Either by design or conviction the leaders of the Sulfur Bay movement adopted the cult to keep their disciples happy and contented. Each Friday evening a delegation come to Ipekel from all the villages who have given allegiance to these leaders. The groups play guitars and sing and anyone who feels like dancing does so. All the songs are supposed to spring from John Frum, first to a daughter of one of the leaders who in turn taught them to the others. But the high point of the year in Sulfur Bay comes on February 15. John Frum designated this day as the time for annual celebrations. Rehearsals start a month or so beforehand and by the appointed day all villages have prepared dances and skits which are often re-creations of old legends.

The most important part of the event is the military parade. Between eighty and one hundred men are chosen from the followers of the movement. They put on trousers and paint USA in bright red on their chests. Holding bamboo rifles with red painted tips for bayonets they drill in a double column under the orders of a drill sergeant. They are hoping, perhaps, that through some sympathetic magic the Americans will return quickly.

Many stories exist that link the John Frum movement with America. One of the pre-cult legends says that all of America's power stems from a pre-World War II raid when a U.S. aircraft flew into the crater of the Yasur volcano. From deep inside they pulled up the powerful being from whom they derived their power. It was John Frum who was responsible for the Americans' arrival in the war; he was a good friend of an American foreman who worked with the Tannese. This foreman told them not to take any of the things the Americans left behind as he was going to give them new things. He had the ability, with John Frum, to be in several places at once. In any quarrel he was always on the side of the Tannese. Some maintain that he told them to keep their identity discs because half of their wages were being held for them in America. Sometime in the future they would be able to recover this money if they presented their identity discs. Many natives also believe that this foreman and John Frum will someday return to Tanna and bring with them all the things the islanders desire.

The John Frum cargo cult has persisted for more than 30 years. Missionaries and administrators have stopped trying to wish it away and are beginning to face the realities of the situation. Although many Europeans still try to ridicule the obvious irrationalities of the cult, it is now becoming clear that only by understanding the essential nature of the Tannese can any change, apart from despair, be brought about.

Pentecost Islanders
New Hebrides

122

Female clan members dance
behind a Bunlap villager
covered in red spots to indicate
his seniority. Conch shells are
blown before killing a pig, the
climax of the ceremony.

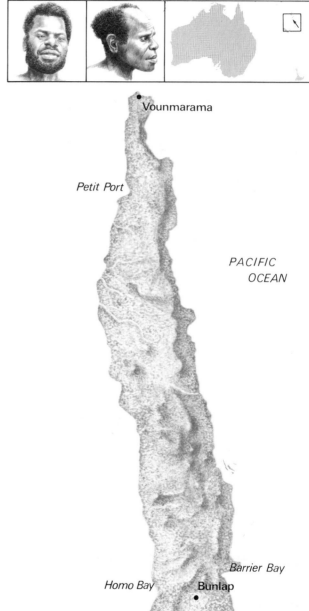

Vounmarama

Petit Port

PACIFIC
OCEAN

Barrier Bay

Homo Bay   Bunlap

0   10   20 km.
SCALE
0   10   MILES

As a ritual, a test of courage and a sheer spectacle, the 'land diving' performed by the villagers of Bunlap (in the Pacific island of Pentecost) is without parallel among the practices of other South-Sea islanders. It can, perhaps, only be compared with the parachuting and sky-diving activities that attract some 123

A liana is fastened onto each ankle of the diver by two assistants. To absorb the jolt of the falling body, launching platforms will collapse.

A Bunlap, his arms held back against his chest — a sign of courage — swings his weight forward to set off his land-dive of a novice's 40 feet.

bold spirits in the Western world.

Bunlap lies on a steeply escarped hillside overlooking the sea on the south-east of the island in the New Hebrides group. There are some 250 Melanesian natives in the region who still live in the way of ancient traditions; about 130 in Bunlap and the rest scattered in four hamlets less than an hour's walk away. Although all males over 15 have had some contact with Western culture, these people compose the last socially viable pocket of non-Christians on the island. Most of the other natives have been assimilated into one of the many Christian sects that proliferate throughout the Pacific.

There is a legend that explains the beginnings of the land dive. A man once had a wife whom he mistreated. She ran away on several occasions only to be caught each time. However, on one occasion she climbed a banyan tree. Sighting her, the man began to climb the tree to catch her. Unknown to her husband she had attached lianas to her ankles. Just as he reached out to capture her, she jumped. Seeing the woman fall unhurt, but unaware of her trick, the man jumped after her and was killed.

The spirit of the land dive is very much alive throughout the year. For instance, a land dive chant is sung when a newly constructed canoe is pulled from its construction site in the bush to the sea. It is especially alive for the young boys who play at land diving constantly. They dive into the sea pretending they are diving from the land dive tower. They build land dive towers to scale, from 4 to 8 feet high, complete with jumping platforms. After having invited the girls to dance and whistle encouragement, they mimic a land dive ceremony by letting a piece of wood fall off the various platforms. At other times young boys climb on their fathers' shoulders and jump off in the land dive position as their fathers hold on to their ankles.

The construction of the land dive tower has been revolutionized by the use of axes and machetes, which have completely replaced stone-cutting tools in the last 50 years. In previous times a tall, strong tree, usually a banyan, was chosen to serve as the tower. A tall façade

was built against this tree, but not reaching beyond the top. It required over a month to complete the tower and the jumping platforms. Now the construction takes about two weeks and starts with the cutting of large logs. These are dragged to the tower emplacement with lianas by 15 men singing in unison and pulling together. The first man to cut the tree to be used as one of the main vertical supports has the privilege of jumping from the highest platform. However, he may relinquish this honor to one of his brothers or some other male member of his clan.

Once all the large logs are assembled, holes are dug around the central living tree. Then, one by one, these logs are maneuvered into position: some of the men pull on lianas which are attached to the top of the log and strung over one of the branches of the central tree; others lift the log from underneath while still others center the lower end of the log into its hole. Once the main vertical logs are in position work begins on the skeleton of the tower. This is 12 feet square and reaches upwards to 80 feet changing slightly in shape. As the tower rises above the top of the main vertical supports, other logs are added on top of these.

The construction of the body of the tower (as distinct from the launching platform) is a joint effort. While some of the men cut and bring the construction materials, others do the building. A friendly and exuberant atmosphere always prevails at the tower site; often there is singing, and some of the men dance on the tower, pretending that they are going to jump but catching themselves as they begin to fall. If it is noticed that the tower is beginning to lean, a long liana, sometimes over 120 feet long, is tied round one of the vertical supports. The other end of this liana is wrapped around a suitable stump, anchoring the land dive structure to the slope behind it.

While working on the tower the men sometimes cook for themselves. It is forbidden for women to come near the tower site during the construction. After the building begins all sexual relations cease until the jump is over. If

124

(Opposite) By leaping from a platform 65 feet above the ground, a Bunlap demonstrates his courage. A perfect dive will ensure an excellent yam crop.

Grass-skirted girls watch a
12-year-old Bunlap boy diving.
Success is achieved when the
top of the diver's head brushes
the ground without injury.

this taboo is broken, it is believed that someone might be seriously hurt while jumping, or perhaps even killed. Different levels of the tower are named after parts of the body. One is called the upper thigh; the next, the stomach; then the pectorals, and so on up to the culminating platform's level, which is called the top of the head.

The construction of each launching platform is the work of the man or boy who will jump from it. He is usually assisted by friends but the responsibility is his. Work on the platforms begins after the completion of the body of the tower. They are constructed on the ground then pulled into position at the desired level, to jut out some 3 feet from the body of the tower. Each one is supported from underneath by three thin branches, which are meant to break at the end of the jump to help to absorb the shock. Once the platform is in place each man selects two jumping vines. One end of each of these is securely fastened to and around the platform while the other end is left to dangle downwards. The head must touch the ground if courage is to be proved. The prospective jumper therefore calculates very closely the length of the liana and the excess is cut off. The lower ends of these two lianas are then cut into strips, which are left to dangle until it is time for the individual to jump. When the men are ready the lianas are pulled up and each one is fastened around an ankle.

Several days before the jump, the area in front of the tower is cleared of all bush. All stumps are removed from the landing area and the ground is softened by turning it over with machetes. The night before the jump most of the men stay near the tower to soften the ground by breaking all clumps of dirt to a depth of up to 10 inches. They also stay to prevent any 'poison men' from pushing an evil object into the ground which would bring harm to the jumpers. On the morning of the jump all males go to the sea for a ritual wash. Afterwards they rub coconut oil on their bodies. Each individual then decorates himself with leaves suited to his rank and his fancy. A set of matched pigs' tusks, fastened stem to stem with the tips curving outward, is tied around the neck.

The men and women start dancing near the base of the tower shortly before the first boy jumps. The dance is a very simple back and forth movement, three steps to one side and three to the other. The women whistle between their teeth while the men do the singing. The songs are periodically punctuated by yells and shouts in unison. During all the land-dive ritual the sexes never intermingle. When someone is ready to jump the dancing intensifies and the songs and whistling grow louder to give courage to the jumper, sometimes at the latter's request.

When a man is ready to jump he separates from the dancers. He climbs the tower to his platform. Two assistants wait for him. They bring up the lower end of the lianas attached to the platform. These are securely tied around the jumper's ankles. He then walks out to the end of his platform. Often the men are scared at this stage,

Like the weight of a pendulum, a Bunlap man swings after his head has brushed the ground. Sometimes the lianas break — but after taking the strain.

trembling at times. But a man may back out without shame and another will quickly take his place. When a man is ready to jump everyone becomes quiet. Sometimes he makes a short speech during which he can talk about anything which troubles him. This might be, among other things, marital difficulties, problems with his pigs, or sickness brought on by someone who wished him ill. At the end of the speech the dancing, singing, and whistling starts again at a higher pitch of intensity and enthusiasm. The jumper then pulls some leaves from his belt and throws them into the wind. If a girl picks one up it means that she wants to sleep with him.

Just before jumping the man claps his hands over his head several times, clenches his fists and draws his arms tight against his chest. With his back arched he then leans forward his feet staying on the platform as long as possible, giving a slight push forward at the last fraction of a second. He then plunges head first toward the ground. Just as his head approaches the softened ground the lianas snap tight and the platform supports break as the tower leans forward slightly. All of this helps to absorb the shock. If the length of the vines has been correctly calculated his head just brushes the soil before rebounding in a graceful arc. As soon as he is still some men rush out to cut the lianas and strip them from his ankle. The jumper's triumphant entourage includes the women of his clan but never his wife, since, if she joined in, everyone would ridicule her for seeming overeager to have sexual relations with her husband.

At times one or both lianas break at the moment of maximum tension, but not without taking up the shock. Sometimes jumpers are slightly hurt, usually with a pulled leg muscle; but after a massage they quickly rejoin the dancers for the next jump. No one has ever been seriously hurt in a land-dive. Throughout the day the jumping continues. One by one the men jump from higher and higher levels. Some men jump several times. The excitement builds up until the last man jumps from the highest platform.

After his jump everyone dances on the landing area in front of the tower. About one week after the jump the lianas anchoring the tower are cut. The top heavy tower falls forward uprooting all the supports. The logs and branches of the tower are used for firewood, and the people of Bunlap, fortified and refreshed by this impressive ritual, return to the routine of their daily life.

The land-dive ceremony is closely associated to the agricultural cycle of the yams. The natives believe that the land-dive guarantees a good yam crop. There is also a direct relationship between the texture of the first yams unearthed at harvest time and the strength of the lianas which will be tied to the ankles at the time of the jump. Both respond similarly to the amount of rain and sunshine received in the previous months.

127

A diver has his cramped leg manipulated. Despite the apparent dangers of land diving, only two such incidents arose in 59 dives.

A successful diver (above center) flings his arms in jubilation while his friends hold him aloft and kinswomen dance round in admiration.

Mbotgote
Malekula Island

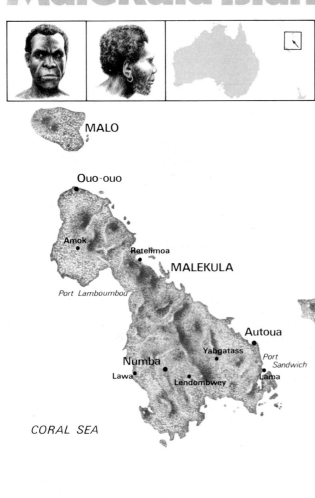

MALO

Ouo-ouo

Amok

Retelimoa

MALEKULA

Port Lamboumbou

Autoua

Yabgatass

Numba

Port Sandwich

Lawa

Lendombwey

Lama

CORAL SEA

SCALE
0   10   20   30   40   km.
0   10   20   30 MILES

the typhoon season, with pulpy banana stems and palm branches. The distinguishing feature is the rounded front and back of the huts, with the back section often reserved for the pigs.

Taro, a starchy tuber, is the principal crop, but yams and other tubers are also cultivated. All gardens are enclosed by strong wooden fences to keep out the voracious domestic and wild pigs. With under-population and an abundance of wildlife, hunting and fishing are more important here than elsewhere in the New Hebrides. Fat shrimps and eels are usually killed in shallow streams with a machete – a 30 inch knife. Flying foxes and pigeons are hunted with bows and arrows. Wild pigs are caught by the dogs, and the men finish them off with machetes.

Taro is normally roasted over an open fire. Meat is either boiled, or cooked in a laplap – a dish for which yams or taro are first grated into a paste using the thorny branches of the fern tree, spinach-like leaves and meat are added and then everything is wrapped in leaves and placed in a shallow pit lined with pre-heated stones. More hot stones are placed on top of the package, which is covered with dirt and leaves and left to bake several hours, sometimes overnight.

The men wear the simplest possible garb – a section of banana leaf wrapped around the penis, and tucked under a bark belt. The women wear a grass skirt, distinctive in being short in the front, long at the back, and made from twisted fibers. But if the outward aspects of Mbotgote life are simple, the system of seniority in their society is very complex – and in turn leads to their complex funerary arts and rituals.

Their belief in ancestral spirits has not suffered from the European contact which has affected other peoples of the New Hebrides. To the Mbotgote, life is held in trust from these ancestors – and their fertility and the co-operation of the spirits is assured by the many rituals and ceremonies that accompany every funeral. The scale or grandeur of such funeral ceremonies will depend upon the rank any man or woman achieved in the village *nimangi* hierarchy during his or her life. This achievement will also determine the respect accorded to the dead once they have passed into the spirit world.

Nimangi is a graded society where, through certain rituals, a man rises to higher and higher levels and thereby gains prestige and importance. There is no real chief: authority rests in the hands of elders who acquire influence through their high rank in the *nimangi*. To acquire a grade in the *nimangi,* the villager must first possess a sufficient number of tusker pigs. These are domestic pigs whose upper incisor teeth have been knocked out so that the lower tusk can grow unimpeded in a curve, its tip growing back into the jaw. The size of the pig does not affect its ceremonial value – only the amount of curvature counts. These tusker pigs are also used in the purchase of a wife. The second essential factor in the

The Mbotgote, isolated in the forested heart of the island of Malekula, have preserved a tribal life that is almost untouched by civilization. They are cut off from the coastal regions by swollen rivers in the rainy season between December and May. Occasionally excursions take place to the copra plantations where cash may be earned for such luxuries as axes or machetes. Few Mbotgote tribesmen are attracted by the opportunities that more civilized settlements offer. They have heard of Christianity, but are little affected by it.

The Mbotgote number about 150 living in three villages and a few hamlets in the south central area of the island. Each village has its men's hut and family dwellings, and their construction is similar to those found in other areas in the central part of the New Hebrides archipelago. A steeply sloped palm thatch roof, over a wood frame-work, is reinforced with sections of fern stems and, during

The elongation of a child's head is caused by heavy cloth bindings during the early months of life. It was traditionally a mark of beauty, but today is rarely practiced.

A mother presses masticated taro into the mouth of her year-old daughter. Until weaning at three physical contact between is almost uninterrupted.

acquisition of a grade is the accord and help of higher graded men. To obtain this the younger men usually defer to the wishes of the elders in all matters.

There is a corresponding *nimangi* society for the women. As they are not allowed on the ceremonial ground in any of the villages, the rituals associated with the women's *nimangi* must be held elsewhere. This is usually a cleared area near the cultivated patches, where ceremonies of several days' duration make the construction of temporary shelters essential. Often several kinswomen will take the same grade together. In one of these ceremonies the women have their right front tooth removed. They first spend some ten days without working, eating only soft foods so that the gums become soft. When it is time to remove the tooth they lie flat on their back with a short piece of wood clenched between the teeth. Held down by relatives, a kinsman stands over them and places a short stick on the tooth to be removed. He then hits the other end of the stick with a stone. After several blows the tooth is usually loose enough to be pulled out with the fingers. The stems of certain plants, heated over embers, then plug the gap left by the tooth in order to stem the blood flow.

During the dances that follow, the initiates sometimes carry the skull of a deceased relative whose features have been modelled in clay. This ensures that the spirit of the deceased relative will participate in the ceremony and help her living relatives. At the least, the spirit will not harm them because of neglect. The skull is carried on a short piece of bamboo during some of the dancing and it is nearby when the tusker pigs are killed at the end of the ritual. Beside conferring prestige, the higher *nimangi* grades enable the women to have more elaborate funerary arrangements after they die. And the more elaborate their funeral, the more their spirit will be held in honor by surviving relatives.

On the recent death of a senior man of the village, a ritual began which lasted almost a year. It illustrates vividly the role that funerary ceremonies play in Mbotgote life. His rank assured him a highly elaborate preparation for the after-life. First his body was washed and then daubed with clay. A new penis wrapper and bark belt were put on the corpse, while still in the men's house. Later it was carried on mats and blankets to one of the family huts to be laid out with the head to the wall and feet to the center. Surrounding the body, a 6 inch deep drain was cut into the earth floor. The men then sat in a semi-circle around the corpse wailing, but forbidden by custom from clearing the nasal mucous. The wailing went on for an hour – and as word of the man's death spread, men from the other Mbotgote villages came to weep at his side.

In the tropics it takes only a few days for a body to swell up. When eventually the humers burst out, they flowed into the simple drain. It was then possible to place the body on a funerary stretcher, covered with leaves, on

Women prepare themselves for
the funeral of a poisoned girl.
As a sign of mourning they
paint themselves white with a
mixture of water and ashes.

some rafters just beneath the roof. For a month the body
rested there, high in the communal hut. The women
cooked, the children played, the people slept – all beneath
the shadow of the corpse. The only constraint on normal
life during this period was that loud noise and raucous
talk were forbidden. And during this phase the dead man's
spirit made noises – and even spoke. The Mbotgote
believed that the dead man's spirit was lurking in the
adjoining forest, and was responsible for the combination
of low pitched ululations and raspings which a European
would associate with a bullroarer. The sounds drifted
across the village at dusk or in the hours of complete
darkness – and those who heard the talk of the dead were
forbidden to leave the fenced area surrounding the
family huts. During this month, preparations for the
funeral went ahead – and the ceremonial ground was put
out of bounds to women, and even to men who had failed
to pay in tusker pigs for the right to participate in the
ceremony. They could only approach the ceremonial
ground on the day of the funeral. After this time of lying
in state the body was brought close to the ceremonial
ground, decorated with colorful leaves and with the skull
of a kinsman lying at the foot of the cadaver. The drums
were beaten and the funeral procession entered the
clearing to begin a ritual called the *nemassien*.

First came one of the elders painted in black and
carrying a six-arched bow tied together by cross pieces.
The stretcher followed, borne by four men painted with
red clay. More men followed, carrying yams and *taro* in

woven mats on their backs. Then came the dancers
painted in red and black. The cortège made its way
around the ceremonial drums several times. Finally the
body was placed on a stretcher in the funerary shed. There
it was supported to a height of 5 feet by the walls of the
shed, composed of tall, leaf-covered bamboo poles.
Thirty feet from the ground, crowning the highest pole,
the skull of a deceased kinsman stared out over the scene.

Outside, banyan roots had been fashioned into
additional funerary structures. The bunched roots were
fastened like massive crabs round the trunks of trees
placed in the ground along the edge of the ceremonial
area. They were decorated with the colorful, crimped
leaves of jungle croton, and surmounted with models of
pigeons and flying foxes. These carefully fashioned
figures would – the Mbotgote believed – help the dead
man's spirit fly to the place under the sea. That is the last
resting ground of their people – a land where there are no
hills to climb, no work to be done in the gardens, where
pigs proliferate and there is ample dancing.

Ancient masks were brought from the men's hut, and
placed on stakes in front of the funerary lean-to. This,
the Mbotgote believed, ensured that the spirits of dead
village elders attended the funeral. The masks had curved
pigs' tusks protruding from the mouth, or from the
forehead – symbols of the wealth of the dead man. The
participants danced in front of these masks, and shuffled
around the drums all night. Even driving rain failed to
stop their dance – for the motive was to express respect for 131

Each grade of the village
hierarchy has its own statue.
Carved from the main stem of a
fern tree, this statue is of one
of the lower grades.

Village elder puffs a clay pipe
as he uses coconut-fiber string
to tie palm fronds to roof poles.
The two tusks extracted from
a live boar denote his seniority.

the dead in particular, and the spirits of the village in general. A good funeral flatters and propitiates the spirits. And they, in turn, will give the living Mbotgote tusker pigs, abundant crops, and good health. At worst, a well-performed dance will turn away some of the hostility the spirits may feel to the dead person's descendents.

The night gave way to dawn and yams and taro were piled in front of the funerary shed. Tusker pigs were killed with arrows – sometimes seven or eight arrows, plunged into the tusker's heart, before a machete delivered the death blow. Other tuskers underwent symbolic killing – they, too, subjected to the bombardment of arrows. As the Mbotgote wanted these pigs to live again – perhaps for another ceremony when they would be killed in earnest – the arrows had been blunted. Meat from those pigs which were killed was baked in laplap and consumed over a period of days.

Even with the dancing over and the funeral complete, the dead man needed further preparation for the afterlife. Pigs continued to be sacrificed in his honor. Only when eventually kinsmen secured the required number of pigs could they bury most of the bones under the funerary shed. But not all the bones – the skull was left aside to form the centerpiece of a macabre statue, or *rhambaramb*. The *rhambaramb* was built for the same reason the dances were performed – to propitiate the powerful deceased ancestor whose irritation could lead to bad health or the failure of the crops of the dead man's

descendents. The *rhambaramb* represented the dead man's wealth and prestige at the moment he was struck down.

Every Mbotgote skill went into the fashioning of this effigy. As with other local art objects, it was based on a framework of wood, covered by a mixture of reddish clay and liana fibers. The legs and arms of the *rhambaramb* were made of bamboo, the torso of the trunk of the fern tree. The head was formed by the dead man's skull. Kinsmen labored to make these simple materials into a close model of the deceased. Even a hare-lip was depicted. Spiders' webs were matted and smoked, before being stuck to the clay-daubed skull to represent hair.

When the deceased's figure had been constructed, it was time for his rank to be blazoned. Pig's tusks were placed round the forearms, as symbols of the many pigs the dead man slew in his life-long pursuit of higher social grades.

A very senior *rhambaramb* gets 'extra' heads – small clay faces placed on each side of the *rhambaramb*'s neck, while others were placed on each shoulder and on the figure's knees. Each little face had pig's tusks coming from the sides of the mouth, then curving back into the clay face in the same manner that a pig's tusks curve back into its own cheeks. The Mbotgote have explained the origins of the *rhambaramb* with the myth of a family dispute. The family consisted of five brothers with white skins and superhuman powers. One brother died, and the eldest survivor exerted his powers to resurrect the dead man. But another brother objected and they compromised by creating a *rhambaramb* statue, with the outward aspect of the dead man, but lacking speech.

However the *rhambaramb* originated, it was then placed before the funerary structure. In a semi-circle behind it, beside a low cracked bamboo wall, there were several smaller figures with arms upraised. These represented the deceased's children who had died. Behind the same wall, protruding over the top, there were many masks with long extended eyes, representing other spirits. The final phase of the funerary ritual consisted of a slow moving procession by men covered with many layers of green or smoke-blackened fern. Pieces of coconut meat were stuck on slender twigs into the fern costumes, and tall conical masks or matted spiders' webbing hid the faces of the men who represented spirits.

Two men with their bodies painted half in white and half in red accompanied the fern-covered figures. These two men lashed all the spectators with plant stems so that they would not be frightened by the spirits. The slow procession ended in front of the *rhambaramb* where everyone was given a yam decorated with ginger flowers from the pile in front of the funerary figure. Tusker pigs were then killed for all the spectators and participants – a great feast that marked the end of the funerary ritual. The Mbotgote could again return to normal life – assured of the spirits' benevolent attention, and with an affirmation of the fertility of their people.

Glossary
Peoples of Australia and Melanesia

The indigenous population of Australia is Aborigine; in Melanesia: Melanesians and some Polynesians.

For the last two hundred years the population of Australia has become overwhelmingly European, predominantly Anglo-Saxon.

In Melanesia the population is still mainly Melanesian except in New Caledonia where 45 per cent of the population are Europeans – mainly French.

ABORIGINES

Theories vary on their origin, but they are believed to have migrated from India, Malaya, New Guinea via the Cape York peninsula. Only about 100,000 survive. Except in Tasmania where they are extinct, numbers are increasing. Their height varies. The tallest tend to be about 5 feet 7 inches. In the north they are longer-limbed and smoother-skinned than in the south. They tend to have long, narrow skulls, deep-set eyes, noses that are wide at the nostrils. Hair varies from wavy to frizzy.

They are semi-nomadic hunters and food-gatherers. Men hunt kangaroos, wallabies, emus, game. Women gather nuts, berries, edible roots, wild fruit.

Each local group, or horde, is restricted by boundaries of territory. The horde is a clan or group related by kinship and marriage with women from other hordes. Age and manhood are attributed great importance. There are elaborate and painful initiation ordeals for young men. Government is by an informal council of old men. Tribes are loosely associated linguistic groups of hordes with little social or political cohesion.

Religion centers on mythical ancestors, the creators of natural phenomena on which life depends. Annual totemic increase ceremonies are held to promote the increase of both food and children.

Aborigines travel light. Traditionally they wear only girdles and pubic coverings of opossum wool or human hair. They have no beasts of burden, limited wooden and stone implements and only rough shelters of bark or windbreaks of bushes as housing. For entertainment they like to sing and dance.

MELANESIANS

Melanesians come from mixed Papuan and immigrant stocks. They live in the area from south east New Guinea to the Fiji Islands and south to New Caledonia.

They tend to be short – from 5 feet to 5 feet 5 inches. Heads are long, noses broad and depressed with thick lips, sometimes oblique eyes, skin from dark coffee color to light brown, hair from frizzy to wavy.

They are gardeners. Men clear the forests, plant and put up fences against the wild pig. Women weed, tend plants, dig them up. They cultivate and eat yams, taro, bananas, plantain, sweet potatoes, coconuts, breadfruit, wild sago palm, tobacco and areca nut – for betel chewing, which they enjoy. On the coast they fish.

They live in small villages with populations of 50 to 200, either irregularly planned or with houses ranged along a main street or round a ceremonial ground. Many of them are dominated by the men's house or club-house. Families usually live one to a house. Sometimes a group of families or an entire village cultivate a whole plot – with individual plots marked off with tree trunks.

The basic social unit, the clan, claims descent from a common ancestor. Descent is both patrilineal and matrilineal. There are two principal kinds of spirit – the ghosts of the dead and others; no regular priesthood.

Traditionally men wore a loincloth made from bark-cloth or matting, or a sort of kilt. Women wore skirts made from strips of pandanus or other leaves. Ornaments are occasionally worn through the septum of the nose or as ear-plugs in distended ear-lobes. The Melanesians make pots – which they use for cooking. Much of what they make tends to be highly decorated. They make and play musical instruments, dance and tell mythological tales.

POLYNESIANS

Polynesians are believed to originate from India by way of Indonesia, although there is evidence of admixture from South America. They live in the islands of the eastern Pacific and most of the central Pacific and parts of the western Pacific.

Their appearance varies. Average height is about 5 feet 9 inches. Skin is whitish to dark brown. They tend to be heavy and run to fat with broad, massive faces with a high forehead, large straight nose, full but defined lips, rounded jaw-line, black eyes – sometimes with a slanting mongoloid appearance, wavy hair.

They are fishermen and gardeners and use practically every known method of fishing. With fish the staple diet is taro, yams, sweet potato, plantains, breadfruit and coconut. Traditional houses have just one room with thatched roofs and screened or open sides. Villages consist of irregularly grouped houses, usually built on stout posts, or on a stone platform for men of rank.

The basic social unit is traditionally the extended family. Head of the family is the oldest-born of the oldest-born. The ruling chief of an independent population is the most direct descendant in a senior line from the first-ever head of the family, and ruled one district or island. Genealogies of the chiefs provide connections with the creator gods, the source of their spiritual energy and power, *mana*. There is a pantheon of gods. Stone platforms are used for religious ceremonies.

Men traditionally wore loincloths or kilts of woven fibers. Their arts and crafts are much admired – particularly carving, decorated bark-cloth, dancing and music.

134

ABELAM *Population:* several thousand. Language: Abelam. The Melanesian Abelam live in New Guinea in the low hills and flat land of the Sepik River area. They cultivate root crops and keep domesticated pigs. Their staple crop is yams. They live in small villages. Their ceremonial life is elaborate and centers on the yam cult. They are famed for their carving, engraving and painting.
(pages 70-79)

AIOME PYGMIES *Population:* 8-10,000. Language: Aiome. These pygmies live in the mountains and valleys of the New Guinea highlands at the foot of the Schrader Ranges, about 70 miles west of Madang. Pygmies are rare in New Guinea and this is one of the few known groups. Their average height is about 4 feet 2 inches. They grow root crops, mainly the sweet potato, and keep pigs, their only domesticated animal. They wear scant clothing and live in huts made of bark and covered with plaited leaves. These huts are scattered over the cultivated slopes, each family living on its own piece of ground. Only occasionally are a sufficient number of huts built together to constitute a village. Pygmy men usually have only one wife which is rare in New Guinea. Their women are secluded and are hardly ever seen by strangers.

ALJAWARA *Population:* 5-600. Language: Arandic Aljawara. The Aboriginal Aljawara live in Australia, in the east central desert, in three concentrations; at Lake Nash near the Queensland border, at the McDonald Downs and at the Warrabri Reserve. The majority continue their traditional nomadic hunting and gathering existence but some work on the sheep stations of the outback farmers. These aborigines still practise totemic rituals, although a few have become Christians. They bury their dead, unlike most other groups of Australian Aborigines who place the corpses on tree platforms.

ANIWA ISLAND PEOPLE *Population:* 185. The Melanesian Aniwa Islanders call themselves Numrukwen, and are part of a Tannese tribe. Aniwa is a tiny volcanic islet in the southern New Hebrides. Most of the southern part of the island is a lagoon. The islanders' economy used to be based only on cultivation and fishing but recently has expanded to include the cultivation of copra (coconut products) and oranges for export.

Sweet potatoes and vines are the staple foods. The houses have bamboo plaited walls and roofs made of pandanus or coconut leaves, and are grouped into villages. The biggest social unit is the patrilineal extended family. The islanders are now all Christians.

ARANDA (ARUNTA) *Population:* few hundred. Language: Arandic. The Aboriginal Aranda live in Australia in the arid central desert around Alice Springs. The scant rainfall is erratic and the few waterholes may be dry for months at a time. Originally they were nomadic hunters and gatherers, but now, although a few still continue this way of life, many work on the cattle stations and townships that have sprung up in their territory. They were probably the most sophisticated of the Australian Aborigines. Their eight-section marriage system is probably one of the most complicated in the world. Some Aranda are Christians while others continue their totemic rituals.

ARAPESH *Population:* only a few hundred are left. The Melanesian Arapesh are mountain-dwelling people of New Guinea. Their territory stretches from the mouth of the Sepik River on the north coast to the plains beyond the mountains inland. The coastal Arapesh have a staple diet of sago supplemented by fish. The mountain dwelling Arapesh have a staple diet of taro and lead a much poorer existence. Those living in the inland plains grow tobacco and trade with the Abelam. There are elaborate forms of exchange of pigs and pearl shells. Warfare is unknown. The Arapesh worship ancestral ghosts, and most misfortunes are attributed to sorcery.

ASMAT *Population:* several thousand. Language: Asmat. The Melanesian Asmat live in New Guinea, in a vast tropical rain-forest on the south-west coast of the island. The land is flat and swampy. The Asmat hunt wild pigs, catch fish and shrimps in the numerous rivers that cross their domain. Their staple food is sago, obtained from the pithy stem of the sago trees that grow wild in the forest. They use sago wood for building their houses and canoes. In each village there is a woodcarver who is revered for his skill. Religion centers upon the worship of ancestors.
(pages 64-69)

BELLONA AND RENNELL ISLANDERS *Population:* a few hundred. Language: Bellona and Polynesian. The small coral atolls of Bellona and Rennell lie to the south of Guadalcanal in the British Solomon Islands. They rise vertically out of the sea and inland are covered with dense vegetation. Physically, the inhabitants are Polynesian – that is they have straight hair and light skins. They live by cultivating, hunting and fishing. Their main crops are yams, bananas, taro and coconuts. The smallest social unit is the patrilineal descent group which owns land. Villages are composed of different descent groups. Christianity has overlaid the traditional ancestor worship of these people.

BENA BENA *Population:* 1,400. Language: Bena Bena. The Melanesian Bena Bena live in the eastern New Guinea highlands, east of Goroka. They constitute a language group of 65 named tribes, each of 2-5 exogamous patrilineal clans. Like most New Guinea highlanders they live by cultivating and by raising pigs. Patrilineages group together into village settlements.

BIAK AND NUMFOOR PEOPLES *Population:* a few hundred. These Melanesian islanders live just off the northern coast of New Guinea on the Schouten and Numfoor islands. Their natural resources are scarce and they live by fishing and trading. Their villages lie along the island coasts. They are now Christians but cargo cult movements have long been endemic; they reached a climax during the Second World War, when there was an administrative vacuum.

BUNLAP *Population:* 130. The language contains a strong element of Pidgin. The Melanesian Bunlap live in the south-east of Pentecost Island in a village on the steep hillside. The men wear penis sheaths and the women wear knee-length grass skirts. They cultivate roots and keep pigs: the staple crop is yams. They are noted for their 'land diving,' from platforms over sixty feet high, with lianas attached to their ankles. Their ceremonial and ritual life centers on the agricultural cycle.
(pages 122-127)

135

BIG NAMBA *Population:* a few hundred. Language: Bichelamar – the local variety of Pidgin English. The Melanesian Namba live on the island of Malekula, one of the largest of the New Hebridean islands. The Big Namba live in the inhospitable mountains inland while the Small Namba (Mbotgote) live on the coast. In Bichelamar 'namba' means penis wrapper and the Big Namba were so called because of the voluminous bright purple penis wrappers they wear, to distinguish them from the Small Namba who wear smaller banana leaf penis wrappers. Living inland they have tended to have less contact with the Europeans than the coastal people. Life continues much as it has always done except for the advent of iron tools and firearms. They are still suspicious of strangers.

CHIMBU *Population:* 60,000. Language: Chimbu, but some Pidgin spoken. The Melanesian Chimbu live in New Guinea occupying the high valleys of Chimbu, Waghi and Koronigl, where the mountains rise to 15,000 feet. They live by cultivating, mainly the sweet potato, which is grown up to 8,000 feet. The valleys are densely settled, and while some Chimbu have become well acquainted with Western ways and ideas, others have had very little contact indeed with white people. As in many highland New Guinea societies men and women do not sleep in the same houses. Some people are either semi-Catholic or Lutheran but many still worship ancestors in the traditional manner.

DANI *Population:* 75,000. Language: Dani. The Melanesian Dani are a language group living in New Guinea. They inhabit the fertile Grand Valley of the Baliem River, in the Snow Mountains of Irian Barat. Men wear long penis sheaths reaching to the shoulder and women wear a loose skirt of fiber coils. The basis of their economy is cultivation and keeping domesticated pigs. Their staple crops are sweet potatoes and taro. The Dani villages are scattered over the slopes of the mountain side. They consist of men's houses and separate houses for the women and children. The main Dani activity is warfare, although casualties are low. They still worship ancestral ghosts.
(pages 92-99)

DARIBI *Population:* 3,000. Language: Daribi. The Melanesian Daribi live in New Guinea on a volcanic plateau on the River Tua, south of Mt. Karimini. In this lushly forested area they cultivate, hunt and gather forest foods. Their staples are bananas, yams, taro and beans. Clans are the basic unit of their society – they tend to move about according to the political situation of the tribe.

ELEMA *Population:* 20,000. Language: Elema. The Melanesian Elema live on the swampy south coast of New Guinea, along the Orokolo Bay which is 100 miles long. Their economy is based on sago cultivation and other crops include yams, taro and bananas. They live in villages under local 'Big Men' (non-hereditary headmen). Most of the population is now Christian. The society suffered greatly in 1919 with the 'Vailala madness' – a manifestation of cargo cultism. The villagers built large platforms scattered with presents in the hope of attracting cargo which they believed would fall like manna from heaven. If they worshipped the God of the white man, they could have the material goods the white man enjoyed – or so they believed.

FORE *Population:* 13,000. Language: Fore. The Melanesian Fore live in the rain forests of the eastern New Guinea highlands due north of Mt. Wanevinti, at a height of 4,000-9,000 feet. They live, like most other highland New Guinea peoples, by pig raising and cultivating. They have recently come to the attention of the medical world on account of a debilitating viral disease, peculiar to the society of the South Fore, known as *kuru* – or locally, 'the laughing death.' A victim of *kuru* is slowly deprived of all physical powers. Ever since cannibalism has ceased there has been a considerable drop in the number of *kuru* sufferers. It is believed that ritual cannibalism caused the spread of the disease and this belief is upheld by the work done by medical scientists and anthropologists on the genealogies of victims. The Fore live in isolated patrilineal hamlets. Men sleep in the male house; women and children occupy separate houses. There is a great deal of

136

tension between men and women. Religion is centered round the worship of ancestral ghosts.

FUTUNA ISLANDERS *Population:* a few hundred. Language: Pidgin and an indigenous Polynesian language. Futuna Island in the New Hebrides allows settlement only along the coast because of the long spine of uninhabitable rock running down the center. The people are Polynesians of Tongan descent. They have light brown skin and wavy hair. Their economy relies on fishing. Christianity and traditional ancestor worship exist side by side.

GADSUP *Population:* 6,000. Language: Gadsup. The Melanesian Gadsup live in New Guinea near Kainantu in the eastern central highlands. Like other New Guinea highland societies they depend on cultivation and pig-raising for subsistence.

GAHUKU-GAMA *Population:* 8,000. The Melanesian Gahuku-Gama live in New Guinea, near Goroka in the central highlands. They cultivate root crops and keep pigs; the staple is the sweet potato. There are several tribes included under this term but they share a uniform language and culture. At one time there was a lot of inter-tribal fighting. Land is owned by patrilineal sub-clans. Men and women sleep in separate houses. On ceremonial occasions such as pig-killing festivals and initiation ceremonies sacred flutes are played.

GARIA *Population:* 2,500. Language: Garia. The Melanesian Garia live in New Guinea, in the Madang District. They inhabit the low but rugged mountain ranges between the Ramu River and the Naru River. The economy is based on shifting agriculture. The staple crop is taro. The Garia have lived in villages since the 1920s when much of the traditional life of the tribe broke down. Men sleep in separate houses from their families.

GIBSON DESERT ABORIGINES *Population:* 3,000. Language: Pitjantjara. The Aborigines of the Australian Gibson

Desert wander over a vast tract of arid and inhospitable land in a perpetual search for food and water. They hunt wild-cats, emu and kangaroo, and they gather wild fruits, roots, lizards and grubs. Staying only a few days at one camp they are always on the move. They continue their totemic rituals and it is vital for every boy to be circumcised at initiation, if he wants to remain a member of the tribe. **(pages 48-53)**

GIDJINGALI *Population:* 300. Language: Gidjingali. The Aboriginal Gidjingali live in Northern Australia on an aboriginal reserve in Arnhemland. Traditionally they pursued a nomadic hunting and gathering existence – fish, game etc. Now they live on a government settlement and many are wage laborers.

GIMI *Population:* about a thousand. The Melanesian Gimi live in the eastern highlands of New Guinea, in the Labogai District, near the Papuan border. One of the main features of their culture is a highly developed ceremonial life, with singing accompanied by dramatic farces.

GURINDJI *Population:* a few hundred. The Aboriginal Gurindji live in the arid Central Desert of Australia. They were traditionally nomadic hunters and gatherers but are now settling down on cattle stations and are beginning to intermarry with other tribes. Some Gurindji are Christians but many participate in the traditional totemic rituals.

GURURUMBA *Population:* 700. Language: Gururumba. The Melanesian Gururumba live in New Guinea in the Upper Asaro Valley, near Goroka. This is a high and fertile valley in the eastern highlands. They grow root crops, tobacco, and coffee and keep domesticated pigs. They live in villages. There is an elaborate system of gift exchange, the most important items are pigs, exchanges of which take place with great ceremony. The tensions in this society are such that it is not infrequent for a man to go off into the bush for a few days with the material goods of his fellow villagers which he will destroy. **(pages 88-91)**

HULI *Population:* 25,000. The Melanesian Huli live in New Guinea in the fertile basin of the Tagari River in the southern highlands. They cultivate root crops, mainly the sweet potato, and raise pigs. Homesteads are scattered over the mountain slopes, each family living on its own particular piece of land. Men and women sleep in different houses.

JALÉ *Population:* 100,000. Language: Jalé. The Melanesian Jalé live in the highlands of New Guinea, east of the Baliem Valley in West Irian. They cultivate mainly the sweet potato and also taro, yams, millet, sugar-cane and bananas. They gather lizards, mice and frogs, and hunt tree kangaroos, giant bats and cuscus, and keep domesticated pigs. They live in villages comprising a large men's house and with a cluster of smaller family huts built around it. The Jalé spend a lot of time in warfare. There are rituals at birth, initiation and marriage. **(pages 80-87)**

JATÉ *Population:* 20,000. Language: Jaté, with dialectical differences according to groups. The Melanesian Jaté live in New Guinea, about 10 miles north-east of Mt. Wanevinti in the central highlands. Jaté economy is based on pig-raising and cultivation. They live in patrilineal corporate groups, giving mutual help for housebuilding, cultivating land, etc. The men own sacred flutes. There is tension in the relationships between men and women.

KAKOLI *Population:* 11,000. The Melanesian Kakoli live in the western highlands of New Guinea, in the Upper Kaugel Valley – one of the highest regularly inhabited valleys in the world. The people gain a livelihood by cultivating sweet potatoes, taro and maize in the valleys and on the terraced slopes. Higher up in the mountains white potatoes and greens are grown. Pigs and chickens are kept. Clan-owned territories and villages are scattered through the valley. The society is noted for its many lifelong bachelors.

KAMANO *Population:* 12,000. Language: Kamano. The Melanesian Kamano live in the central New Guinea highlands near Kainantu. In this society women do most of the work of cultivating. They sleep with their children away from the men and relationships between men and women tend to be strained. They live in small patrilineal hamlets.

KAPAUKU *Population:* 45,000. The Melanesian Kapauku live in New Guinea in the rugged central highlands of West Irian, where the peaks rise to 14,000 feet, out of the lush and fertile virgin forest. In appearance they are shorter and stockier than the coastal peoples. For a livelihood they cultivate roots and keep pigs. Their staples are sweet potatoes, sugar cane, taro and they also catch crayfish, frogs, water insects and dragonfly larva from the rivers. They live in rectangular plank houses roofed with thatch or bark. Men and women sleep in different houses. Kapauku religion is elaborate in ceremonial and emphasizes secularism and individualism.

KIMBERLEY TRIBES *Population:* 8,000 consisting of about 30 tribal remnants. These Aboriginals live in Australia and once roamed the Kimberley Plateau, on the north west coast. Nowadays they are concentrated in and around the little towns of the north west coast, such as Wyndham, Derby and Broome. Their traditional nomadic hunting and gathering way of life has been abandoned for menial work in the towns. The tribal headmen have lost control and the old values are being lost. Those who still live in the desert shelter in circular roofless windscreens and go naked. Those who live near the coast have simple huts, and wear European clothes. Most of these Aborigines are now Christians.

They still fish on the coast but use different and modern methods.

KOITA *Population:* a few thousand. Language: Koita; some English is spoken. The Melanesian Koita live on the dry, barren southern shore of Papuan New Guinea in the Port Moresby area. They are largely a fishing people and engage in large scale trading enterprises. Some live in villages outside Port Moresby and others in its suburbs. Most Koita are wage earners.

KOROFEIGU *Population:* 900. Language: Bena Bena. The Melanesian Korofeigu live in New Guinea, in the eastern highlands, east of Goroka. They cultivate and raise pigs. Their staple food is the sweet potato, but they grow a great variety of crops. They live in villages in patrilineal groups. They strongly believe in the polluting nature of women and the superiority of men.

KUKUKUKU *Population:* a few thousand. The Melanesian Kukukuku live in New Guinea in a vast domain of forest and mountain in the Gulf District of Papua and the Morobe District of New Guinea. Semi-nomadic, they are distinguished by their bark cloth capes and sporrans and their reputation for ferocity. Resisting administrative control until the 1930s they used to sweep down from

the hills to slaughter the peoples of the plains. Like most other New Guinea highlanders they cultivate roots and keep pigs. Until fairly recently they were cannibalistic.

KUMA *Population:* a few hundred. Language: Yoowi. The Melanesian Kuma live in New Guinea in the Waghi Valley of the western highlands. Besides cultivating root crops and keeping pigs they trade. Homesteads are scattered over the hillsides.

KYAKA *Population:* 10,000. The Melanesian Kyaka live on the western highlands of New Guinea on the north slopes of Mt. Hagen range, and between the Baiyer, Lai and Ku Rivers. Although they have access to rich forest hunting and gathering they depend almost entirely on cultivating and pig-raising. They have an elaborate ceremonial exchange system. They live in dispersed homesteads, grouped occasionally into small clusters.

LAKALAI *Population:* 3,000. Language: Lakalai, a dialect of Nakanai. The Lakalai – a mixture of Polynesians and Melanesians – live in New Britain on the central north coast, on the narrow coastal plain of Hosking Peninsula. One side is bounded by volcanic mountains and the other by coastal bush. They are physically varied in appearance. For a livelihood they cultivate, and hunt in the forest. Villages are owned by matrilineages. Christianity and cargo cults have overlaid the traditional ritual beliefs and practices.

LARDIL *Population:* 200. Language: Lardil. The Lardil are Australian Aborigines living on Mornington Island, in the Gulf of Carpentaria, Northern Queensland. They live now much as they have always done on a land rich in food resources. Clothing is scant. They gather roots and yams, besides berries, panjas and water lilies, and they hunt wallabies, swamp turtles, ducks, geese, lizards and goannas. They also fish for turtles and dugongs. Traditionally they were semi-sedentary unlike most Australian Aborigines staying in the same camps for several months at a time. Land is owned by clans with unrestricted rights and access to the sea in front. The Lardil are renowned for their dancing. Their only decorative art is the

practice of painting and decorating their bodies.
(pages 40-47)

MAE-ENGA *Population:* 30,000. Language: Enga. The Melanesian Mae-Enga live in the western highlands of New Guinea on the west of the Hagen Ranges. In the lower valleys there is dense rain forest and a high rate of malaria. The most populated parts are the mid-mountain forest zones. The people are small, stocky and dark. They cultivate – mainly the sweet potato – and keep pigs. Their homesteads are scattered through the territory. Religion is centered on ancestral cult worship.

MAILU *Population:* a few thousand. The Melanesian Mailu live in New Guinea along the coast line between Port Rodney and Orangerie Bay. They cultivate, hunt, fish and keep pigs. Their staple is sago. They also live just off the coast on Mailu Island which houses the only potters in the area. Their coastal villages are built on high piles.

MANAM *Population:* 3,500. The Melanesian Manam live on Manam Island, eight miles from the coast of New Guinea. It is the most southerly of the Schouten Islands and is an active volcano. Their economy is based on cultivation. They live in scattered homesteads forming parishes. Men's club houses – one per parish – hold sacred objects like slit gongs and sacred flutes.

MANGA *Population:* 400. The Melanesian Manga live in New Guinea in the Sepik drained valley of the north-eastern sector of the western highlands. Subsistence is gained by cultivating and pig-keeping. Their staple crops are sweet potato, yams, taro and cassava. Religion is centered round ancestral ghost worship.

MANIKION *Population:* 5,000. The Melanesian Manikion live in New Guinea in the mountainous country of the eastern Vogellkop, West Irian. They are nomadic pig-raisers and cultivators who have spread and are further spreading over a large area. There are a few Catholics in the society but traditional religious beliefs are still widely held, especially the belief in the efficacy of black magic.

MARIND ANIM *Population:* a few thousand. The Melanesian Marind Anim live in New Guinea in the swampy land of southern West Irian. They live by cultivating, hunting and fishing. Their staple food is sago. They live in patrilineal villages. Their traditional philosophy of life is maintained, especially the impressive dramatization of creation myths, but there is an overlay of Catholicism and cargo cultism.

MBOTGOTE *Population:* 150. Language: Mbotgote. The Melanesian Mbotgote live on the heavily forested island of Malekula in the New Hebrides. The men wear penis sheaths made of banana leaves and the women wear grass skirts short in front and long at the back. Basically they are cultivators; taro is the staple crop, but they also hunt (flying foxes, pigeons and wild pigs), fish (shrimps and eels) and keep domesticated pigs. They live in villages composed of a men's hut and the family houses. Authority rests with those elders who have attained a prestige position during their life. The Mbotgote, also called Small Namba, believe in ancestral spirits and carry out elaborate funeral ceremonies.
(pages 128-133)

MARING *Population:* 7,000. Language: Maring-Jiani. The Melanesian Maring live in New Guinea in the rugged and heavily forested area south of the River Ramu in Madang District. The economy is based on cultivating and pig-raising. Their staple foods are sweet potatoes, yams and manioc. Women do the heaviest work of the cultivating while men go to, or plan, war.

MEKEO *Population:* a few thousand. The Melanesian Mekeo live in New Guinea in a fertile area in the central division of Papua. The land is subject to seasonal flooding. Traditionally they lived by cultivating and fishing. Their staple food is the yam. Recently wage labor has begun and rice has been introduced as a cash crop. Traditional patterns of social behavior have broken down but villages are still largely formed of patrilineal descent groups. Christianity and cargo cultism have overlaid the traditional ancestor worship.

MELPA *Population:* over 50,000. The Melanesian Melpa are a language group living in New Guinea in the Hagen subdistrict of the western highlands. The group is composed of several fragmented tribes, of about 12,000 each. They cultivate and keep pigs, which, as in most other highland tribes, are used for ceremonial exchange purposes. Their exchange sphere goes outside Melpa: shells from the southern highlands via the Waghi Valley are exchanged for pigs, stone axes, salt and decorating oil (carried in long bamboo tubes). Trade takes place on a family basis, rather than at markets. Tribal warfare finished after 1946 and now each tribe only unites for a pig-feast or a spirit cult. During the ceremonial exchange known as 'moka' the people wear lots of paint and ornaments. Each group tries to outdo the other in its gifts of shell valuables and pigs.

MENDI *Population:* 33,800. Language: Mendi. The Melanesian Mendi live in New Guinea in a rugged mountain valley about 25 miles long in the southern highlands of Papua. The land is 5,000-7,000 feet high. These people are very small (the average height for men is 5 feet high and for women 4 feet 8 inches). Their staple food is the sweet potato. Members of the same patrilineages live together in villages.

MOTU *Population:* 2,500. Language: Motu; some Pidgin spoken. The Melanesian Motu live in New Guinea in the poor, dry coastal area of Port Moresby. They fish and trade overseas and some are wage laborers depending on the distance they live from Port Moresby. They live in villages or the Port Moresby suburbs and although much of the traditional culture has been lost they still have village feasts and ceremonies.

MUDBARA *Population:* very small and declining. The Aboriginal Mudbara live in the arid western desert of Australia near Wane Hill. Some are still nomadic hunters and gatherers but others work on government mission stations. The Mudbara living in the desert still go naked. They are in danger of becoming absorbed by the Walbiri to the south. Most are now Christianized but some still participate in totemic rituals.

MUNDUGUMOR *Population:* 1,000. The Melanesian Mundugumor live in the eastern highlands of New Guinea in the Sepik Valley on the Yuat tributary. The land is high and fertile. Traditionally they were headhunters and made continuous warfare on the people of the swamps. They trade tobacco, areca-nut and coconuts with the swamp people who supply them with pots and baskets. The people are suspicious of each other and live in isolated homesteads with their wives and children. These homes were traditionally palisaded against attack from members of their own tribe. They had a reputation for ferocity. Social organization centers on the matrilineal line, and there is no clan organization.

NEW CALEDONIANS *Population:* 35,000 indigenous Melanesian inhabitants. Language: there are about 30 dialects of New Caledonian – a Melanesian language. New Caledonians are Melanesian in appearance with dark skin and crinkly hair. Women are extensively tattooed to enhance their beauty. Traditionally, subsistence agriculture and fishing were the bases of the economy but in this century many New Caledonians have become wage laborers on French plantations, and have been drawn into the European economy. Before the coming of the Europeans the New Caledonians had what was claimed to be the only state-like society in Melanesia. Villages were, and are still, laid out according to plan. The houses have conical thatched roofs. Authority was in the hands of hereditary chiefs. Ceremonial life was very elaborate and the masked dances spectacular, with masks reaching to the ground. Most people are now Christians. Traditional religion was animistic.

NGAING *Population:* 800-900. Language: Ngaing. The Melanesian Ngaing live in New Guinea, on the north east coast near Saidor. Sharp ridges, gorges and swift flowing rivers cut across the country. Trade is the basis of the economy and betel nuts, wooden bowls, and bark cloth are exchanged for clay pots, siasi beads, salt, fish and marine products. Movement is very difficult and slit gongs are used for communication. Yams, taro, and bananas are cultivated. The Ngaing settle in villages. Traditional ancestor worship has been overlaid with Christianity.

NUNGGUBUYU *Population:* 300. The Aboriginal Nunggubuyu live in Australia in south east Arnhemland and on Bickerton Island. Some still continue the traditional hunting and gathering existence while others work on sheep stations. Religion is still largely totemic; each person has his own country to which his totem is linked. There are many taboos concerning totems.

OROKAIVA *Population:* a few hundred. Language: Binandele. The Melanesian Orokaiva live in the forested division of the Northern Division of Papua. Their economy is centered on cultivation and pig-raising. Their staple is the sweet potato. They live in scattered homesteads. A lot of body

ornamentation is worn – feather headdresses, nose-rings, bones and shells. The Orokaiva resort to sorcery rather than warfare for the redress of wrongs.

PINTUBI *Population:* several hundred. Language: Pintubi, but Pitjantjara and Pidgin are also spoken. The Aboriginal Pintubu live in the western desert of Australia, now mainly on the Haast's Bluff Government settlement at the western end of the Macdonnel Ranges, although they once roamed a great area of desert. Traditionally they were nomadic hunters and gatherers. Now most work for white cattle owners, as stockmen, fencers, and gardeners, getting food from the ration house on the settlement. Recent intermarriage with other Aborigine groups is resulting in a loss of tribal identity. Both Christians and pagans are still initiated in the traditional manner. Those who remain uncircumcized are liable to be treated as outcasts.

PITJANTJARA *Population:* several thousand. Language: Pitjantjara. The Aboriginal Pitjantjara live in the Central Desert of Australia, around Alice Springs. Some are still nomadic hunters and gatherers, but many are settled on Government stations at Haast's Bluff and Areyonga, where they intermarry with other tribes. Some are Christians and some continue traditional totemic rituals.

RAO-BRERI *Population:* several thousand. Language: Rao-Breri. These adjacent Melanesian peoples live in New Guinea, along the lower Ramu Valley 80 miles west of Madang in the heart of a swampy plain. They have been studied very little. Settlement is in villages. Christianity has been superimposed on indigenous ancestral cultism.

RONI *Population:* 350. The Melanesian Roni live in New Guinea, in the Wurup Valley near Mt. Hagen in the western highlands of New Guinea. They have plenty of land on hills going up to 8,500 feet, forest resources and flat dry ground. They cultivate and raise pigs for a living. Their staple is the sweet potato. Lately they have been encouraged to plant tea as a cash crop. Traditionally, land belonged to the clan over which the family had rights to cultivate – families never owned the land themselves. Religion is centered on ancestor worship.

SAN CRISTOBAL ISLANDERS *Population:* several hundred. Language: Kahua. San Cristobal is one of the largest of the Solomon islands. It is 100 miles long – a rugged, mountainous island with a densely forested interior. The Melanesian islanders, who are dark and crinkly haired, depend on fishing and subsistence agriculture. Recently coconuts have been planted and copra is produced commercially. Traditionally they had exogamous matrilineal clans. Adultery is now more frequent than in other societies.

SIANE *Population:* several thousand. Language: Siane and some Pidgin. The Melanesian Siane live in New Guinea in the eastern highlands. They are short, compact people. They cultivate and raise pigs for subsistence. Land is owned by the individual – whereas in many highland tribes clans hold the land. The Siane inhabit villages on the ridges of the precipitous mountains, separating the Goroka plain from the Waghi Valley, about 6,200 feet up. Their religion is centered on ancestor worship.

SIUAI *Population:* 4,700. Language: Motuna. The Melanesian Siuai live in the southwest corner of Bougainville Island in the Solomons. They occupy the Great Buin plain, which is dissected by numerous rivers. They are very dark-skinned people with crinkly hair. They practise shifting agriculture: the staple is taro, but they also

141

grow sweet potatoes, coconuts and areca-nut palms. They hunt in the forests, especially for wild pigs. They also fish and keep domesticated pigs. The Siuai live in villages built on piles, and in the cultivated areas there are hamlets and scattered houses. Most households have two houses, one in the bush and one in the village. Since contact with the Europeans, iron tools have replaced the stone and bamboo ones. They decorate their bodies with elaborate patterns. They also carve wooden objects.

SMALL NAMBA *see* **MBOTGOTE.**

SOLOMON ISLANDERS *Population:* 190,000 Melanesians. Language: Tribal languages and Pidgin. The Solomon Islands lie to the north of the New Hebrides. They rely on fishing (the bonito fish is most prized) and cultivating for a subsistence livelihood. The islanders retained their traditional way of life until the Second World War more or less intact, but then there were serious disruptions as Guadalcanal Island became the scene of serious fighting between the Americans and the Japanese. This was the cause of the Moro cult – a socio-religious movement involving a large proportion of the population.
(pages 108-115)

TANGU *Population:* 2,000. Language: Tangu. The Melanesian Tangu live in New Guinea about 15 miles inland from Bogia Bay on the north coast of Madang District. The knot of steep and forested ridges rises sharply from the downland of the sea coast. Tangu men wear wide waistbelts of woven pandanus, over petticoats of soft banana fiber. They still continue their traditional cultivating, hunting and foraging livelihood although some Tangu men are wage laborers. Their primary tools and weapons are the digging stick, axe, adze, spear and knife. Their homesteads are raised on stilts and formed into settlements of four or five, round a central feasting place. Communications take place by word of mouth or slit gong. Some of the traditional ideas and beliefs of the Tangu have now broken down, although there is still a body of belief that commands their loyalty. Some Tangu are Christians or at least nominal Christians, and many have been baptised but cling to their traditions.

Cargo cults took a strong hold on this society, but are less widely held today.

TANNESE *Population:* 12,000 on the island of Tanna. Language: Pidgin is the lingua franca. The Melanesian Tannese are mainly farmers; their most important crop is the copra extracted from the coconut palms the missionaries persuaded them to grow. In the extreme south-west of the island the people live as they did traditionally in small hamlets. They have tended to reject European standards in their recent participation in the John Frum cargo cult. They believe that they will return to a golden age promised by John Frum if they resume their traditional life. Many men have cast off their European clothes and adorn themselves with leaf penis-wrappers again.
(pages 116-121)

TASMANIAN ABORIGINES An extinct people *Population* was 2,000 at the first count in 1804. The last full-blooded Tasmanian died in 1876. Language: there were thirteen known vocabularies of the Tasmanian language. The Tasmanian Aborigines were palaeolithic hunters and gatherers like the Australian Aborigines but they were less technologically advanced. They went entirely naked, their bodies decorated only by scarification. The coastal groups ate shellfish and inland they hunted kangaroos, wallabies and opossums. This diet was supplemented by grubs, plants and wild root vegetables.
(pages 54-57)

TCHAMBULI *Population:* 500. Language: Tchambuli. The Melanesian Tchambuli live in New Guinea about 180 miles from the mouth of the Sepik River, on a lake flowing into the Sepik by two rivers. They are fishers and traders. Fish and shell money are exchanged for the sago and sugar-cane of the lowland people. The common currency is green snail shells. They live in small hamlets near the lake on the edge of Tchambuli Mountain. There are men's houses, women's houses and ceremonial houses, all built on high posts. The ceremonial houses are decorated with ceremonial heads from the past. The Tchambuli always preferred obtaining their heads from criminals and orphans rather than having to go to war to get them. Their society is organized into two

halves, or moieties, consisting of several clans. Iron tools have replaced the traditional stone ones.

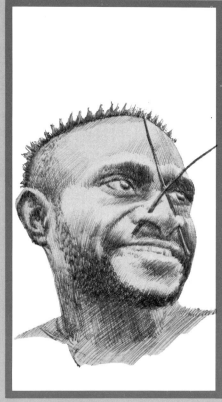

TELEFOMIN *Population:* 1,000. The Melanesian Telefomin live in New Guinea on the headwaters of the Sepik River, on the border of West Irian and Papua. They cultivate roots, their staple food being taro. They inhabit valley villages. Husband, wife and children live together – unlike most highland communities. There is tribal unity only in time of war and then the 'Big Men' emerge as leaders.

TIFALMIN *Population:* 500-600. The Melanesian Tifalmin live in New Guinea in the central mountains not far from Telefomin, and in the upper reaches of the Sepik River. The men wear simple penis sheaths and the women wear short grass skirts. Nose ornaments are elaborate. Tifal men have three holes pierced in their noses through which they pass stone, bone, or bamboo nose pins, pig's tusks, cassowary quills or pearl shell disks. Necklaces and pendants are also worn. The economy is based on the cultivation of root crops, especially taro, sweet potatoes, sugar cane and tobacco. Domestic pigs are kept and eaten as also are dogs. Digging sticks are the only tools used. Men also hunt – wild pigs, cassowary, marsupials and game. Women and children collect eggs, grubs, beetles, tadpoles, small lizards, fruits and fungi. Scattered hamlets form the only kind of settlement. The light wooden houses are arranged around a bare dancing ground. Men sleep apart from the family houses. Missionaries have now penetrated this part of New Guinea and much traditional belief is starting to disintegrate. The Tifal still attach great importance to magic. Musical instruments include drums, bamboo harps, flutes, and simple musical bows.

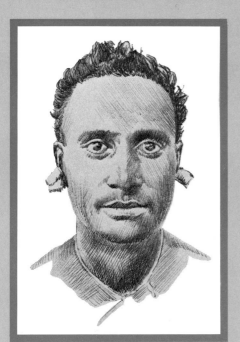

TIKOPIA *Population:* 1,200. Language: Tikopia, Pidgin. Tikopia island is to the extreme southeast of the British Solomons. The Tikopia are Polynesian in appearance with wavy hair and light skins. They have more affinities with Samoans and Tongans than Melanesians. The traditional subsistence economy of cultivating sago and fishing continues in spite of a move towards wage labor on the plantations of the Russell Islands. Tikopia traditionally was a chiefly society with a clear-cut social organization. Most are Christians but traditional ancestor worship continues.

TIWI *Population:* 900. Language: Tiwi. The Tiwi are Aboriginal Australians living on the adjacent islands of Bathurst and Melville, 30 miles from the north coast of Australia opposite Darwin. Unlike most other Australian Aborigines the Tiwi hunt and gather off a fertile land. The rich forests offer wild game in plenty besides wild roots and fruits. The Tiwi used to go almost naked, save for penis sheaths for the men and rough aprons for the women. Today most men wear loincloths or even trousers and women wear skirts. Most roam the bush for food but some young men now go to work in Darwin. The Tiwi continue their old ritual ceremonies, although many of them have become Christians.
(pages 58-61)

TOARIPI *Population:* 5,000. Language: Elema. The Melanesian Toaripi live in New Guinea along the coast in the eastern part of the Papuan Gulf. They cultivate and keep domesticated pigs. They live in large villages, consisting of men's communal houses and the houses for women and children. The men's houses have sacred objects. Christianity has been superimposed on the traditional beliefs in supernatural powers. Periodically there are waves of cargo cultism.

TOLAI *Population:* 40,000. Language: Kuana. The Melanesian Tolai live in the Gazelle Peninsula of New Britain, near Rabaul. Cocoa and copra are grown for exports and the coastal people fish. These are the most acculturated people in New Guinea. Their villages have elected councils. Nearly all Tolai are Christian. They are also the most wealthy indigenous people in New Guinea.

TORAU *Population:* 600. Language: Torau. The Melanesian Torau live in the British Solomon Islands, on the east coast of Bougainville, north of Keita. They are cultivators, mainly of the sweet potato. They live in villages in swampy regions near the coast. These people have declined in numbers rapidly over the last 150 years.

TROBRIAND ISLANDERS *Population:* 12,000. Language: Trobriand. The Melanesian Trobriand Islanders are culturally closer to New Guinea than to the Melanesian islands. Their domain of coral atolls lies just off the eastern coast of Papuan New Guinea. Their economy is based on agriculture and fishing and the rich soil of the islands supports a dense population. Their staples are yams and taro. They are also expert wood-carvers and basket-weavers. They live in small villages which are grouped into districts of varying size. Their elaborate ceremonial life centers on the 'kula' exchange system and the annual yam harvest.
(pages 102-105)

USURUFA *Population:* 900. Language: Usurufa. The Melanesian Usurufa live in the central New Guinea highlands, north of Mt. Wanevinti. They are cultivators, women doing the routine work, while the men fight. Patrilineages own sacred flutes and associated tunes. Relationships between men and women are strained.

WALBIRI *Population:* 1,500. Language: Pitjantjara. The Aboriginal Walbiri live north-west of Alice Springs in the Central Desert of Australia. Traditionally nomadic hunting and gathering people, some now work on cattle stations and live on settlements. Those who live traditionally still live in four communities each tied to a section of land. They practise totemic rituals. Men have an age-grading system based on common circumcision seasons. As in many other desert Aborigine groups the

143

dead of the Walbiri are placed on tree platforms. But the Walbiri also later bury the bodies in anthills – a unique feature of their society.

WALPARI (NJALIA) *Population:* 300. Language: Pitjantjara. The Aboriginal Walpari live in Australia round the government settlement at Yuendumu, 200 miles north-west of Alice Springs. Now they are settled on government missions or work for cattle owners. Some are Christian and some practise totemic rituals.

WARRAMUNGA *Population:* a few hundred. Language: Warramunga, Pidgin. The Aboriginal Warramunga live in Australia, near Philip Creek in the Central Desert. Traditionally they were nomadic hunters and gatherers but this is giving way to wage labor for Europeans and settlement. Their religion is still mainly totemic.

WIK-MUNGKAN *Population:* several hundred. The Aboriginal Wik-Mungkan live in Australia on the western side of the Cape York Peninsula, Northern Queensland, round the Archer, Kendall, Holroyd, and Edward Rivers on the fringes of a native reserve. The low-lying country of swamps, lagoons and waterholes is useless to the whites, but valuable to the Aborigines. They hunt seawater fish, dugong, turtles, possum and gather fruits and honey. The Wik-Mungkan believe their clan's own ground emanates power and therefore has a sacred value. They paint their bodies with red and white clays in elaborate decorations which have many mystical meanings.

WOGEO *Population:* 1,000. Language: Pidgin and Wogeo. The Melanesian Wogeo live on one of the Schouten Islands off the northern coast of New Guinea, opposite the mouth of the Sepik River. This tiny island, 15 miles in circumference, is the most northerly of the group. With a constant heavy rainfall the vegetation is luxuriant. The people practise canoe fishing and cultivating. Their staple crops are taro and bananas. The people are varied in appearance owing to centuries of racial admixture. Their everyday dress is simple:

144

men wear loincloths and women wear petticoats in simple colors. On ceremonial occasions the men wear feather headdresses, turtle-shell forehead plates, woven waistbands, armlets, collars, and headbands. They also wear hair dye. A community of villagers will join together for many ceremonies, especially the initiations. The Wogeo carve wooden figureheads for their houses, and make bark paintings.

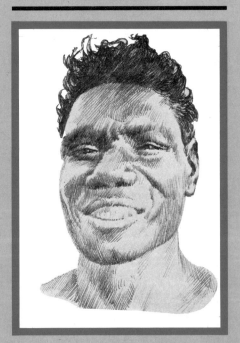

YULENGOR *Population:* 300. Language: Yulengor. The Aboriginal Yulengor live in Australia in the wild and remote bush of Arnhemland. Most get a livelihood by cultivation: some work on boats, along the coast. Patrilineal clans form groups which share a common marriage system and religion. Religion is centered on the practice of totemic rituals. In ceremonial life elaborate totems are made and body painting and cicatrization is common. They also paint on bark cloth.

All population figures are approximate.